# CONTEMPORARY EMBROIDERY

## EXCITING AND INNOVATIVE TEXTILE ART

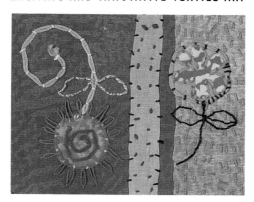

# Contemporary Embroidery

## EXCITING AND INNOVATIVE TEXTILE ART

### ANNE MORRELL

*'Scissors can acquire more feeling for line
than pencil or charcoal.'*

MATISSE

STUDIO
VISTA

**A STUDIO VISTA BOOK**

First published 1994
by Studio Vista
(a Cassell imprint)
Villiers House
41/47 Strand
London WC2N 5JE

Distributed in the United States
by Sterling Publishing Co., Inc.
387 Park Avenue South, New York, New York 10016–8810

Distributed in Australia
by Capricorn Link (Australia) Pty Ltd
2/13 Carrington Road, Castle Hill, NSW 2154

**British Library Cataloguing-in-Publication Data**
A catalogue record for this book is available from the
British Library

ISBN 0-289-80105-2

Typeset by Litho Link Ltd, Welshpool, Powys, Wales
Printed and bound in Slovena by Printing house DELO Tiskarna
by arrangement with Korotan Italiana, Ljubljana

To all the contributing artists,
with many thanks for their help

# Contents

9 *Acknowledgements*

11 *Introduction*

### The Artists

17 Renie Breskin Adams USA

21 Irén Balázs HUNGARY

25 Polly Binns ENGLAND

28 Lloyd Blanks USA

33 Emilia Bohdziewicz POLAND

38 Janet Bolton ENGLAND

42 Jo Budd ENGLAND

46 Helen Daniel ENGLAND

51 Sarah Denison ENGLAND

56 Maria-Theresa Fernandes USA

59 Lissy Funk SWITZERLAND

62 Nicole Gaulier FRANCE

64 Pam Gaunt AUSTRALIA

68 Nicola Henley EIRE

73 Agneta Hobin FINLAND

76 Lillevi Hultman SWEDEN

80 Jan Irvine AUSTRALIA

83 Louise Jamet CANADA

87 Waltraud Janzen GERMANY

90 Alice Kettle ENGLAND

94 Susanne Klinke GERMANY

98 Janet Ledsham NORTHERN IRELAND

101 Tom Lundberg USA

105 Jane McKeating ENGLAND

109 Anne McKenzie Nickolson USA

112 Lee Malerich USA

116 Sylvie Ollivier FRANCE

119 Heikki Orvola FINLAND

123 Tilleke Schwarz NETHERLANDS

126 Lynn Setterington ENGLAND

130 Barbara Lee Smith USA

134 Rose Marie Szulc AUSTRALIA

138 Anna Torma CANADA

142 D. R. Wagner USA

148 Verina Warren ENGLAND

151 Martel Wiegand GERMANY

154 Alexa Wilson SCOTLAND

157 Inez Züst-Gericke SWITZERLAND

# Acknowledgements

THE AUTHOR would like to thank the following for their help and advice: Karen Burns, Christa Thurman, Maija-Leena Seppälä and Beatrijs Sterk.

The author and publisher would like to thank the following: all the artists for their contributions; information for Lissy Funk from the catalogue 'Lissy Funk: A Retrospective', organized by Christa C. Mayer Thurman, The Art Institute of Chicago, 1988.

The author and publisher have made every effort to credit individual photographers and would like to thank the following for permission to use their photographs: Lech Andrezejewski and Teresa Szymomowicz (p. 35), Jean-Pierre Beaudin (pp. 83–5), Robert di Fronco (pp. 142–3), David Hobson (p. 27), Ola Husberg (p. 78), Indav (pp. 119–22), Maria Major (p. 138–40), James Newell (p. 92), Norfolk Museum Services (p. 44), Jerzy Sabara (p. 34), Paul Seheult (p. 39), Barbara Lee Smith (p. 132), Mark A. Smith (p. 131), Steinkamp and Ballog (p. 130), Terry Waddington (pp. 46–7, 53, 69, 105, 128), Stephen Yates (pp. 25–6, 38, 40, 42–3, 48–9, 51, 52, 54, 90–91, 106–7, 126–7, 149).

# Introduction

THIS BOOK is about the different approaches, aims and techniques involved in the production of non-functional, embroidered pieces. It cannot include all the many fine embroiderers working at this time, but it does reflect the variety of ideas, emotions and individuality behind the work that is currently being produced. The pieces described range from those that keep to tradition and rules to those that break some, if not all, of the conventions. The emphasis, throughout, is on stitch and fabric manipulation, as well as on the use of other textile techniques.

The book looks at work being produced by artists who have made embroidery their main method of expression. On the whole, these tend to be women: of the thirty-eight artists whose work is shown here, only four of them are men. The contributors, from many countries, have written something about their work. The selection of those artists included is necessarily a personal one. However, this is the first time that there has been such a wide-ranging survey of contemporary embroiderers and, of the many talented people whose work has been examined, it represents a balance of the different means of expression, techniques, forms of representation and so on that are currently being explored. It is evident that there are as many ways and reasons to make embroidery as there are artists.

This selection of artists shows a diversity of approach and use of embroidery to develop ideas through into fabric, thread and other relevant materials and processes. Yet they all have, certainly in their writing, much in common.

Some of the work is very clearly evocative of the country in which the artist lives or originates from or was educated in – that is, there are influences in the imagery, approach and techniques. Maria-Theresa Fernandes and Anna Torma show in their work the effect of major changes of location on their lives. All the artists are recognized as individuals rather than as coming from a particular place, and the maker is known, which has not always been the case when studying historical pieces. However, the place in which the artist works often has a profound influence on their embroidery, as it does for Finnish artist Agneta Hobin.

There is a variety of sources of inspiration: for instance, the use or not of drawing and photography – a contrast would be Jo Budd and Helen Daniel. Certainly for many – Pam Gaunt, for example – their work addresses auto-biographical concerns: there is a need to express feelings and develop methods to describe them. Irén Balázs talks of some of the reasons for the changes that have developed over the years in her work. Alice Kettle says that when looking back she can 'trace a logical evolution over several years'. The major objective is to communicate feelings and ideas, the work being a form of expression and communication.

Much of the embroidery produced today has universal appeal, due to world-wide communications. Travel, books, TV and exhibitions have all played their part in accelerating the speed of information exchange.

However, while images and ideas are easily accessed from anywhere in the world, some techniques seem to be more popular in some countries – for example, canvas work (needlepoint) in the USA, as evidenced by the work of Lloyd Blanks and D. R. Wagner.

Embroidery encompasses many different techniques which involve fabric and thread, a needle or sewing machine. It is used to decorate evenly woven, netted and other fabrics. It is added from the back or front of the fabric and involves negative-space and construction techniques, as well as being part of edges, hems, seams or fastenings like buttons. In a creative approach, techniques are adapted and developed with the artist's needs and motivation. The work of Nicole Gaulier, for example, is carried out in only one type of stitch.

Embroidery has its roots in basket-making, mat-making, weaving and sewing, and Renie Breskin Adams shows work that links some of these processes. Embroidery has been limited for some time to being the decoration of textile fabrics (and sometimes other materials like leather) by means of a needle and thread (and sometimes fine wire). If embroidery found its way from the area we today call China, it is thought to have started as a quicker way of achieving intricate and curved lines and shapes on a small scale which would have taken a longer time through weaving. Some embroidery has emerged from needlework, a basis of sewing, to decorative needlework. Physically, it has now become a very flexible medium. Stitches can be put in at will, with the directness one gets with drawing, the stitches acting as marks on the surface.

Technical descriptions can be endless, but what is certain is that there is no set process. For example, the work can be dyed before, during or after stitching.

The use of collage by painters earlier this century was certainly a linked breakthrough which embroidery was waiting for. Fabric collage allowed the move from a practical, decorative, illustrative role to a medium for self-expression with fabrics.

For a variety of reasons, sometimes to quicken a process or to achieve the effect required, embroidery is combined with other techniques and materials. Such an approach has long been in use traditionally, and today we link it particularly with printing (Nicola Henley), dyeing (Helen Daniel), painting (Lillevi Hultman) and spray techniques (Barbara Lee Smith and Jan Irvine). (I have not included examples of fibre art or tapestry weaving in this survey.)

Embroiderers, like anyone else who makes artefacts or takes part in a particular activity, frequently ask themselves why they do it. The answer for each person is obviously personal, as the artists in this book demonstrate. They tended to feel, though, that if it was necessary to talk about it, theorize about it, then there was no need to do it. Lissy Funk says she feels that 'Words can destroy a delicate concept that is still coming into being.' Interestingly, though, Waltraud Janzen uses embroidered writing in her pieces.

It is difficult to work without a context. For most, work could develop in a number of directions: focus and accident can determine which choice is made, but a final statement may never be resolved. Producing work is not always possible, particularly if one has nothing to say. For the embroiderer, surely making is an intellectual activity as well as a technical one. The danger of being seduced by the process is understandable. Fabric and thread are familiar to us all, as we have them in our everyday surroundings. They are pliant and enjoyable to handle and to work with, and these are perhaps the reasons why artists are attracted to them. Sylvie Ollivier says that, for her, 'Some embroideries are wonderful encounters with particular fabrics.'

The scale of the fabric, thread and stitch may remain the same whether the work is on a large or a small scale, and this has its effect on the dialogue between the embroiderer and the viewer. Small pieces pull viewers in, to look closely, to become aware of the processes employed in making the mark. The larger piece can push them back, to be able to see the whole. This concern affects the stitching in works by Jan Irvine. Of course, much is left to the viewer to interpret and imagine, though words can act as a guide to help understand the work if the artist is not present. Rose Marie Szulc particularly aims to make work that is understandable and approachable by the general public.

There are a variety of reasons for talking about work

which may or may not include the artist. Discussion about a piece of work can confirm or change the artist's and the viewer's belief in what he or she is looking at. The work is open to interpretation. Often, words are needed to help us to understand what has been produced, and this book should help us to understand something of what the artists are saying. The work does not lose its meaning if the viewer does not understand what the artist intended. For two people to look at the same thing and it to appear as a different concept to each of them does not mean they are not looking at the same thing. After all, how things seem is not always how they are. What is seen is reliant on previous experience and this, together with personal attitudes, influences how it is understood. Certainly Emilia Bohdziewicz is very aware of the viewer and says of her work, 'It has a presence and staying power in the mind and memory of the viewer because of the multiple interpretations.'

For the artist, the final piece of works is often the realization of an idea through chosen media using certain techniques and skills. For artists like Heikki Orvola, the making of the embroidery is as important as the final results.

How well the piece works depends, to a greater or lesser extent, on the way these component parts have come together: the realization of what was in the mind and the reality. In order to understnd the relationship between the mind and the reality of what has been produced, a lot of us seem to need the help of words.

Many artists write about the influence and place of colour and light, and here we have individuals expressing different ideas. For example, women's issues are important for Louise Jamet, symbolism and messages for Irén Balázs. On the other hand, there is, very deliberately, no particular message in the works of Nicole Gaulier or Sarah Denison.

For a number of artists, tradition and folk art are perhaps where their work is rooted: good examples would be Renie Breskin Adams, Janet Bolton, Janet Ledsham, Tilleke Schwarz and Lynn Setterington.

Nature and places are the inspiration for many, including Verina Warren and Alexa Wilson.

Issues can be incorporated too. For example, Inez Züst-Gericke started to embroider because she saw embroidery as a counterpoint to 'pollution in art';

Louise Jamet sees sewing and embroidery as a celebration of women's work; and Lee Malerich wants to challenge the viewer directly with her 'R' and 'U'.

Embroidery can accommodate a variety of scale and there is no longer any need to stay within a frame. We can not only exploit familiar techniques, like folding, wrapping and stitching, but also include activities with cloth like slitting (see, for example, the work produced by Polly Binns).

There are not many basic or new ideas; the same ones keep recurring, but they can be put over in a new way so that viewers and makers are able to see again and afresh. We are often bridging the past and future in work we make today. Janet Bolton and Janet Ledsham have looked at patchwork, Renie Breskin Adams makes raised and detached parts in her works, reminiscent of the stump work (raised work) produced in England in the seventeenth century.

Certainly, there is a need for new ideas and talent to replace, progress and push; otherwise people become too used to what they see. Today it would seem we need to re-present, often shock, to keep the audience looking. Many artists reject the thought that they are creating and feel rather that they are creating experiences; the work is a kind of interpretation. For most, it is necessary to be imaginative – imaginative about ideas and how to use them. Ideas are something we all have and use. For those producing visual art, ideas are communicated by visualizing. The chosen media and process are not important in themselves, but are simply the means by which we communicate, opting for those which suit us the best. Some of the artists in this book work in other art forms as well as embroidery.

It certainly shows in work if the preoccupation has been with the media and process and there is no underpinning idea. It is sometimes difficult for visual artists to discuss their ideas – it can be non-productive to talk about it rather than to think it through – but talking and writing can help to clarify and progress ideas.

As is indicated by pieces currently being produced, there are many ways of directing one's work. There is no right or wrong approach; rather, one is aiming for the confidence to push and develop an idea towards the solution that one is seeking. Confidence to believe in one's own ability is very important. However well meant and helpful suggestions by others can be, they at times undermine confidence and deflect ideas from the control of the artist.

Appropriate research and disciplined thinking are some of the methods that can add to confidence. This is a simple description of the intense dialogue and the self-searching which, over a period of time, one has to struggle with in order to have something to say, even before sorting out how to say it.

For many of the artists, embroidery as a form of expression came from their childhood or early education. Certainly, many were not 'trained' in embroidery and moved from other arts – Emilia Bohdziewicz from interior design, Jo Budd and Alice Kettle from fine art and painting. For some, there are other areas of activity, and embroidery is just one form of expression – for example, Heikki Orvola and D. R. Wagner.

The time taken to embroider, the length of time to conceive the idea, are judged differently by different artists. For example: Jo Budd, '. . . the element of time in the making is part of their quality . . .'; Lissy Funk, 'The process of creation is long and tedious . . .'; Tom Lundberg, '. . . the slow, digestive ritual of creating . . .'; Jane McKeating, 'I love the change of pace between different techniques . . .'

Studio and working conditions vary too. Lissy Funk has a studio with assistants helping in the making, whereas Jane McKeating uses the dining room of her home, sharing it with her family.

Similarly, decisions about finishing the work within a frame or presenting and conserving it are approached differently: Lynn Setterington has no frame, yet the frame is an integral part of the work for Lloyd Blanks, Janet Bolton and Verina Warren. Lloyd Blanks uses information from conservators to conclude the work; conversely the materials used by Janet Ledsham are fragile. As she says, 'The only deterioration is perhaps in colour quality, and this is part of the natural process and is fundamental to the principles of my work.'

---

The measurements are given in the order of height, width and, where appropriate, depth

# THE ARTISTS

# Renie Breskin Adams

I FIRST STUDIED textile arts as a university student, in weaving and other techniques of fabric construction. I later discovered embroidery, a process that has given me a greater freedom from technical constraints in developing my pictorial imagery without abandoning my favorite structures in constructed fabrics. The relationships between techniques of embroidery and textile construction interest me. For example, darning is weaving; couching is identical to warp wrapping or coiling; the chain stitch is identical to the crocheted chain; the buttonhole stitch is identical to knotless netting. The first time I embroidered, in 1978, from my point of view I was attaching knotless netting to a backing. I

*'High-Stepping at the Beach', 1985. 11 × 12 × 1 in (28 × 30 × 2.5 cm). Detached buttonhole, needle-weaving, satin, couching. Knotting and crocheting form the outer frame*

*'Blue Birds of Happiness', 1980–90. 31½ × 34¾ in (80 × 88 cm), detail. Knotless netting construction. The stitches loop through each other as in the detached buttonhole stitch but with no attachment to a backing*

'Goodbye, Sylvia', 1990–91. 29⅝ × 22⅞ in (75 × 58 cm). Detached buttonhole

learned later that I was detaching the buttonhole stitch.

I love fabric and use the materials and structures of the fiber artist, but I feel, like a painter, I must spend a lot of time sketching, drawing and painting. They provide a quick and spontaneous means of finding form – line, shape, texture, color – for my subject matter, which is usually whimsical portraiture. I follow my sketches closely when I'm embroidering, retaining their painterly form and spontaneity during the slow and deliberate process of translating them into fiber structures. For me, material and structure are subordinate to my pictorial image. Like a painter, I want to transform the fabric.

I imagine that my primary motivation in making my embroideries is similar to that of Victorian women who used embroidery or other painstaking textile techniques to record their family histories. This disciplined and beautiful manner of telling our stories is a means of affirming our lives. In my case the need is primarily psychological. I find it very therapeutic to objectify my feelings about life and give them distance in aesthetic, symbolic form and structure.

I start with a sketch, usually in colored pencil. Often I make marks with my pencils that suggest needle-weaving, satin stitch and/or detached buttonhole. Then I make a cartoon of the shapes and trace this onto my fabric. I use cotton canvas and usually a variety of cotton threads. My pieces range in size from about 5 to 40 in (13 to 102 cm) square. In the small works I use sewing threads, embroidery flosses, small perle cottons and small weaving cottons. In the larger works I incorporate wools – knitting worsteds, weaving yarns and tapestry yarns. I collect many, many colors, mixing different strands of yarn.

I sit at a table and surround myself, on the table and on the floor, with boxes of bobbins and spools of threads. Depending on the size of the work and the threads, I may strand from three to twenty threads through the needle to create color textures. While I'm working, I may have five or so needles of threads going in my work at the same time, trading them off as I work within a single passage.

The stitches I use most often are detached buttonhole, needle-weaving, couching and 'satin' stitch. I put the latter in quotes because it is often erratic in structure – surfaces built with little lines of thread that shift and change direction. Occasionally I omit the backing fabric, doing passages of detached-buttonhole stitching started on a crocheted chain rather than attached to a backing. I pin these little shapes to a pinboard that has my cartoon on it. As the shapes grow and meet each other, I stitch them together. The resulting fabric is similar to knotless netting or tightly worked needle-lace. I also incorporate crocheting and double half-hitching (a macramé knot) in my pieces, most frequently in the decorative borders and frames. Often in the decorative framing I raise my embroidery by overlaying stitches, stuffing with small cords and yarns, and constructing 'flaps' of detached buttonhole stitches or needle-weaving.

# IRÉN BALÁZS

AFTER GRADUATING from college I painted and exhibited pictures for more than ten years. I applied leaves of trees, pieces of thread and prints of lace patterns to the pictures; later I started to use the textile itself. Painting gradually disappeared; instead of putting on a thick layer of paint, it was enough to crumple a piece of textile to make it protrude out into space. This method of moulding provided me with a challenging task for years. But I had to find the organizing principle, the circle of ideas that this plastic invention could express. I found the answer in folk art.

'Amorphous Patterns', 1987. 39½ × 39½ in (100 × 100 cm). Linen and cotton

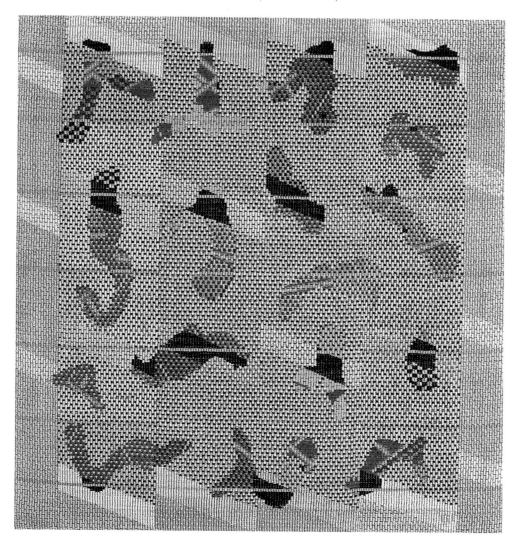

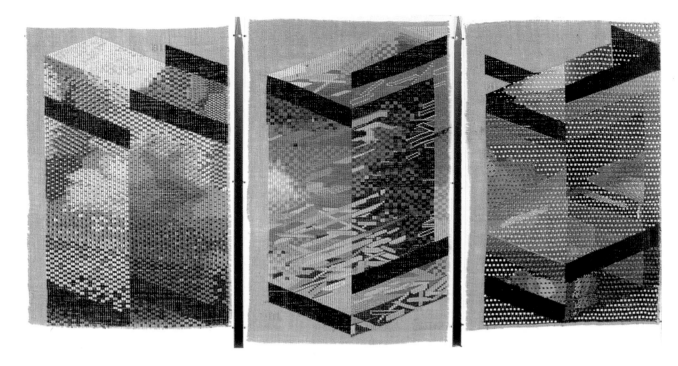

'Reflections 1, 2, 3', 1988–9. Each panel 31½ × 20 in (80 × 51 cm). Linen and cotton

'Reflections 1', detail

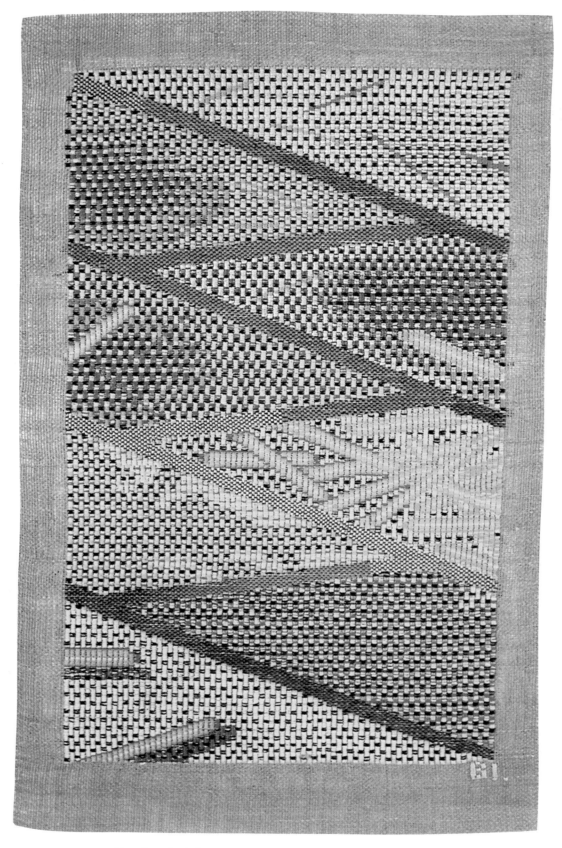

*'View from the Air'*, 1988. 31½ × 20 in (80 × 51 cm). Linen and cotton

Folk art objects and their ornamentation are message-carrying signs. They are messages that were used with the same meaning for thousands of years; forms and colours that had condensed into signs from motifs or nature. They are stylized signs of the sun, the moon, animals and plants. I made use of these signs. There were times when I started to doubt whether these symbols were so obvious for everyone else.

I produced large-sized rustic pieces, using jute, hemp, flax, strings, ropes and cords. Sometimes I also applied coloured embroidery to this raw mass, either to emphasize the plastic effect or to weaken it. The pictures became bigger and bigger, demanding larger and larger spaces for themselves. They were only able to exercise their real effect on the walls of museums. This was the reason why the pieces and the idea itself started to get alienated from me. I had to take a new standpoint, but this only came about gradually.

I made my first flat piece in the 1980s. I realized the importance of colours in this kind of work. Now I cover loose, basic materials with dense chain stitches, and I also get into the depths of the material, as I did when I painted. I halt fine transitions with hard, black, sloping lines. If I repeat transitions and scales in a regular pattern, fictitious spaces, space illusions, open up on the flat surface. On these seemingly – as far as their effect is concerned – infinite surfaces I embroider the motifs for fire, water, earth and sky. I have been working within this circle of ideas for years; one piece grows out of another. After years of redefining, only colour and rhythm remain to keep up their feedback with nature.

I do not make graphic cartoons because, considering them as drawings, I would be endlessly trying to work out the best ways to meet the criteria of drawing. Instead, after primary consideration, I embroider evenly spaced points of orientation on the material. Then, with another point system, I create the space, and then finally the pattern itself. While working I am counting the points, and I insert the motifs among the points, keeping a special eye on the selection of colours. Recently I have put particular emphasis on raster points. Through this I only demonstrate the bare bones of the scheme. This is the way in which content and composition merge into one unit with the material and the technique.

# POLLY BINNS

Drawing and sampling play a limited role in the development of my work. My inspiration comes from a distillation of many influences – often the observation of very subtle changes in a much loved and visited venue, such as certain beaches in north Norfolk.

Overstrand and Sidestrand are two coastal villages in Norfolk where I spend as much time as I can. I walk the beaches and cliffs and the work is a response to my experience and feelings for the landscape, the sky, light and the delights of the rock structures and strata. I am a great fossil collector.

*'Overstrand to Sidestrand', middle section of three, 1992. 30¼ × 30¼ in (77 × 77 cm).*
*Linen fabric, painted with acrylic. Machine and hand stitched with linen and cotton. Slit*

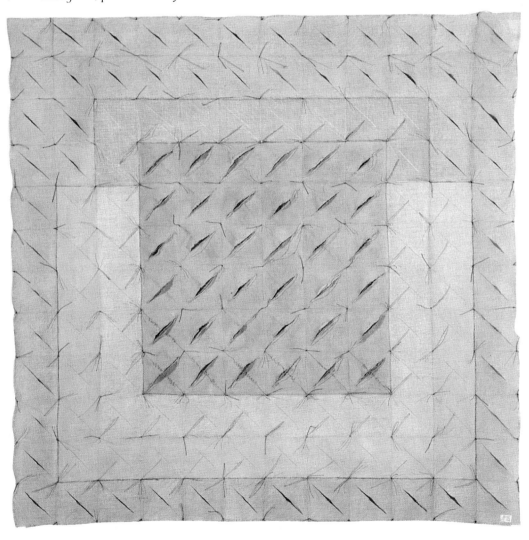

In no sense is the work a response to specifics; it is a distillation of experience.

I aim to capture an elusive 'magic' – that is, a balance between my control and intentions, and what the work gives back to me – so time is spent looking at what is happening in the work in order to realize my creative voice.

I work both in series and singly, and always have several pieces in progress at once. If they begin to group naturally into a series, I develop that potential; I respond to series of three or five.

I go for long periods without any production, but I do spend time thinking between projects. I work around other demands in life, rarely getting an unbroken day. Some elements in my approach reflect this – for example, my involvement in painting and the subsequent drying process. Working ideas start slowly, and with difficulty, and then begin to flow.

I paint with acrylic on to canvas and linen, and use machine and hand stitch methods. I use the zigzag mechanism on the machine to create varied, rhythmic lines and large running stitches diagonally to 100 degrees to fold the work up when it is pleated and manipulated. Other processes of folding, pleating, smocking, cutting and slitting the fabric are in response to the painting and stitching.

*'Overstrand to Sidestrand', detail*

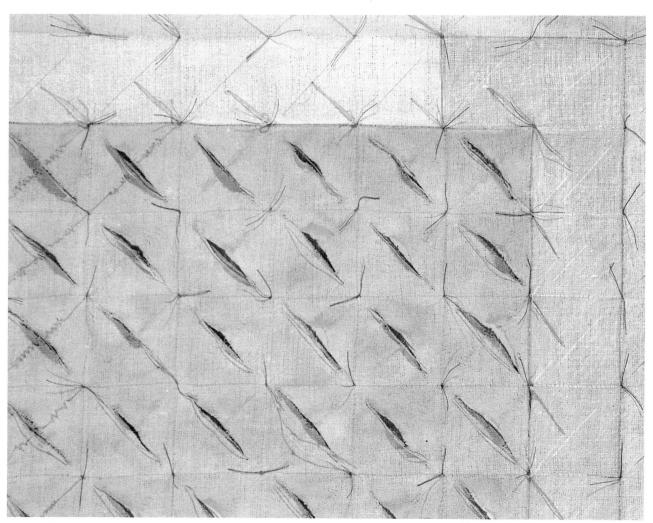

*'Twisted Triangle', 1987. 40 × 43¼ × 5½ in (101 × 110 × 14 cm). Canvas, acrylic paint. Machine and hand stitched, folded and pleated, and 'smocked'*

# LLOYD BLANKS

Aɴᴛʜᴏᴜɢʜ I have lived in New York City for forty years, I still turn to the memories of my childhood on a farm in West Texas for inspiration and subject matter for my canvas works. My pieces are concerned with light and space, horizons and the land as it was, seen under all atmospheric conditions and moods, by night and day, through heat and cold.

I do no drawing or painting on the canvas before beginning a new piece, but merely indicate certain divisions of space. To present to the viewer the message that I bring, I rely on the formal elements of design. I select line, form and color which I feel will contribute most psychologically to the realization of my concept, applying these elements to my personal choice of subject matter.

*'Barren Land', 1990. 16½ × 18¾ in (42 × 48 cm). Canvaswork/wool needlepoint*
*A West Texas landscape: land and sky seen from a farmhouse porch*

*'North Door and Window', 1991.*
*34½ × 18½ in (88 × 47 cm).*
*Canvaswork/wool needlepoint*
*Summer heat on dry land from the*
*interior of West Texas farmhouse*

*'West Texas Sun', 1989. 18¾ × 16½ in (48 × 42 cm). Canvaswork/wool needlepoint*
*On the porch beneath the summer sun*

'Wind and Sand', 1989. 16½ × 18¾ in (42 × 48 cm). Canvaswork/wool needlepoint
Shifting sand in the West Texas wind

Seventeen years after seeing a commercial kit at the home of a friend, I am today working on my one hundred and forty-eighth canvas. Some are small and were completed in two or three weeks, while others are as large as 36 × 72 in (91.5 × 183 cm) and took more than six months to complete, working twelve to fifteen hours a day, seven days a week. I use ten-gauge mono cotton canvas and Paternayan Persian wool, finishing each piece before starting a new one. I average ten pieces a year.

My only stitch is the simple vertical half-cross with a skip-stitch application, which eliminates canvas distortion. Of course, I experiment with needle-mixing of yarns and multiple variations of application for color-blending. In my work there is no piling and clotting of yarns – the reverse side is similar to the front, except for the tying in and tying out.

In working out a system for mounting and stretching, I have relied heavily on information from textile conservators. The mounting boards are ¼-inch (6-mm) white Philippine mahogany (luan), a wood light in weight and low in acidity. After receiving a coat of polyurethane, the boards are hung for a month to air. Then they are given a second coat of polyurethane and hung for another month. Harmful fumes will evaporate, but, as a precaution before stretching, I cover each board with acid-free (non-ligneous) tissue paper and then unbleached muslin. Monel staples are used, since they will not rust or corrode.

My custom frames have a wide lip to cover the hemmed and stapled border to the canvas. The raw wood of the frame is given coats of polyurethane, and strips of museum board (acid-free) are stapled to the inner frame to prevent the canvas border from coming into direct contact with the frame. I screw the custom stretcher to the frame to hold the mounted canvas securely in place. For storage, finished pieces are put into unbleached muslin slipovers for protection from light and dust.

# EMILIA BOHDZIEWICZ

ORIGINALLY, I TRAINED as an interior designer, trying various techniques and combining various crafts. I decided to switch from the role of organizer of vast functional areas to that of producer of articles functioning in those areas. This change was dictated, perhaps, by my urge to work independently, in my own studio. When I made the decision I was an experienced designer and mature artist with a well-defined view of the world. Consequently, my work suggests something broader than a textile training – a different approach and a formal restraint.

I build abstract structures with black linen threads on a surface of natural-coloured woven canvas fabric. My idea is to connect a number of points on the plane with segments of straight lines built of machine stitches or hand embroidery, and this has led me to work on a number of themes. One is the concept of the book or the script. In this, abstract signs, reduced to strokes, seem to be like letters and yet are without the distinct shapes of Latin or Greek characters. They have been composed to make systems varying in rhythm, almost like a printer's template, forming the image of a page as a surface of varying density. A 1979 white book, called 'Eleven Possible Combinations of Vertical and Horizontal Lines', showing just what the title suggests on its textile pages, was 'published' at the 9th Biennale in Lausanne. Formed like a book, the composition encouraged the viewer to turn the pages, as if reading, and follow the graphic dramatic 'plot' and its multi-thread structure, which were built up in the way a novelist would construct a story.

*Book, 'Eleven Possible Combinations of Vertical and Horizontal Lines', 1979. 25 1/2 × 25 1/2 × 4 in (65 × 65 × 10 cm) closed. Machine embroidery*

Over the last decade, I have developed a programme of linear combinations intent on both simplified and very elaborate solutions within a system of signs and symbols placed in soft-textile settings. An example of this is my piece '256 Possible Combinations of the Sign Containing the Eight Elements', which is large in size and reaches the viewer on many levels. It could be considered by some as a simple statement of black machine stitching on white canvas, constructed into a balanced grid. It could be considered as a developing sequence of primary shapes (squares, rectangles, triangles), overlapping with increasing frequency to establish a blend from light to dark, from top to bottom. It could also be a statement about organizing diversity into well-ordered individual modules. It could be a complex intellectual exercise that is progressive within its 256 machine-stitched pieces, which ultimately accumulate to become black – a study in systems. From another perspective it could dematerialize and be read by the viewer as a controlled line drawing. This work is the sum of all these possibilities and ambiguities, and perhaps more, and it has a presence and staying power in the mind and memory of the viewer precisely because of these multiple interpretations.

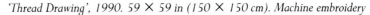

*'Thread Drawing', 1990. 59 × 59 in (150 × 150 cm). Machine embroidery*

'256 Possible Combinations of the Sign Containing the Eight Elements', 1987. 138 × 138 in
(350 × 350 cm). Machine embroidery

'Number 139 out of 256 Possible Combinations of the Sign Containing the Eight Elements',
1990. 24 × 24 in (60 × 60 cm). Machine embroidery on white canvas, the lines produced on
the sewing machine

*'As a Result of Adding', 1991. 98 × 98 in (250 × 250 cm). Machine embroidery on white canvas, the lines produced on the sewing machine*

# JANET BOLTON

I T IS DIFFICULT to isolate influences and inspirations as they come from so many different directions. Because I work with fabrics, the most obvious influence would seem to be the traditional patchwork and appliqué techniques. However, although I enjoy these immensely and have a great love of 'fabric' itself, equal pleasure and inspiration come from works completed in totally different materials. Fine art, folk art, objects, natural forms and landscapes all play a part. Often works completed in different media have a greater affinity to each other than those completed in the same materials.

*'Japanese Paper Flowers II', detail*

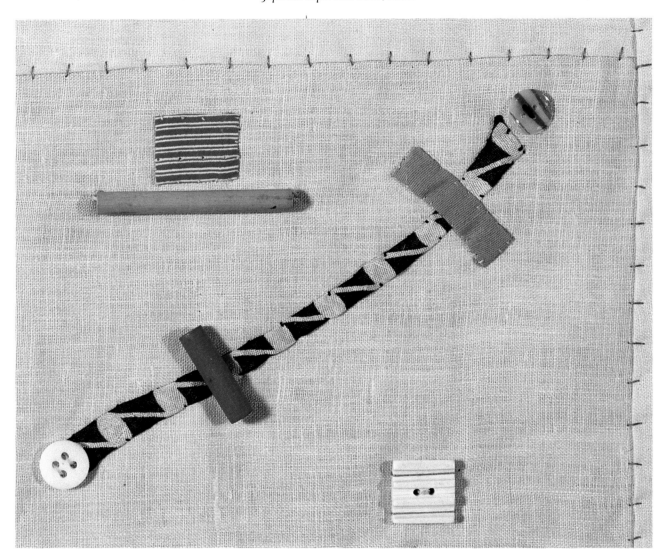

*'Indian Runner Ducks'*, 1990. 8 × 8 in (20 × 20 cm). Cotton fabrics, appliqué

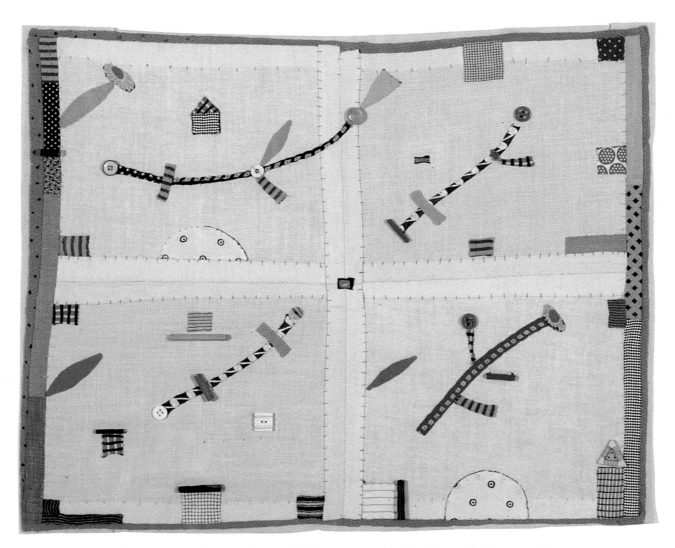

*'Japanese Paper Flowers II', 1992. 23½ × 24½ in (60 × 62 cm). Cotton fabrics, appliqué;*
*sewn by hand, it also incorporates the use of buttons and small pieces of cane*
*This piece is inspired by watching small, flat Japanese paper flowers open out and float in water.*
*It is one of an ongoing series depicting the careful and thoughtful placing of plants in gardens*

At art school a dislike of working with oil paint, combined with an equal appreciation of 'objects', led me away from the traditional Fine Art course to one which included silk-screen printing, lithography and some machine embroidery. Looking back, I knew that none of these areas suited my particular way of working. Seeing the work of Elizabeth Allen, an elderly recluse, at the Crane Kalman Gallery in London helped me to realize what I wanted to do. Like her, I wanted to make simple pictures from pieces of fabric, their impact coming from pictorial balance and composition, not the way in which they had been made, and I wanted to work with fabrics rather than paint.

With a selection of materials and a vague idea in mind, I start to cut, compose and rearrange until a picture begins to emerge. During this process many ideas and possible solutions will be explored, and may be remembered even if not recorded. Often the simplest picture will take the longest time to compose. Some rejected ideas I will keep in mind and use immediately in a different picture around the same theme, so a series of pictures develops. Working on a different theme entirely may suddenly spark off a memory, an appropriateness, and I will return to a theme not explored for many years and rework it. In this manner my work slowly progresses, but in a natural, unforced way. I never find myself thinking, 'What shall I do next?'

Working by hand is very important to me. Turning the edges under when using fine fabrics is as sensitive as producing a drawn line. Time to stop, look and move a fraction of an inch can make all the difference. Laying pieces on and moving them about at all stages is an essential freedom. Using a sewn line as emphasis or to add texture, adding an extra top stitch or maybe one button on a found object at any stage – these are part of the process of building up a satisfying composition.

A couple of years ago I bought a framing machine, and this has proved invaluable. I can now try pictures in frames of different shapes, colours and sizes until I'm satisfied with the appropriateness, and the frame and the picture become one piece of work.

# JO BUDD

I TRAINED AS as a painter and usually work on a large scale, between 159½ × 199 in (4 × 5 m) square, because I enjoy the visual impact of big areas of colour and texture. These pieces take several months to complete, and the element of time in the making is part of their quality, linking them with tapestries or paintings which are worked over and over.

Inspiration is taken partly from the materials themselves, but mainly from my surroundings. My choice of subject matter does not depend on conventional notions of beauty, nor on themes drawn from other artists or cultures. I have produced series of works, for example, on industrial buildings, decaying walls, derelict buildings and boats in dry dock.

*'Dry Dock', detail*
*Lines and edges fascinate me – they can be soft or hard where one colour meets another*

*'Dry Dock'*, *1989–92. 96 × 144 in (245 × 365 cm)*
*This piece was the culmination of a series based on the working boats of Lowestoft. It aims to*
*balance abstraction and mark-making with a strong figurative element*

*'Lowestoft Beach', 1991. 59 × 59 in (150 × 150 cm)*
*I would like viewers to feel that they were sitting in a deckchair, smelling the suntan lotion and*
*hearing the seaside noises*

My feelings about a subject are not completely resolved before I start, and the process of making a picture is one of exploration and celebration of both subject and materials.

A series begins with photographs, from which I then make samplers. These intuitive small pieces allow me to immerse myself in a new subject and to test techniques and ideas. I do not make detailed preliminary drawings, however, preferring to work directly on a large scale, as this gives me more freedom for ideas to grow and change.

The fabrics, which are either ready-dyed or hand-painted with dyes, using sponging and wax and paste resist, are cut freehand and pinned through a vertical backing canvas on to pinboard. This means colours can easily be moved, and I may also collage fabrics on top of one another, making the surface four or five layers thick in places. Dyed translucent fabrics – for example, organdie and muslin – are layered to give colour-wash effects, and I may cut down to reveal layers of colour underneath.

I am fascinated by colour: colour relationships, achieving a balance of colour and tone, atmospheric effects of light and shade, and the emotional language of colour. I enjoy making colours 'work hard', instinctively putting them together in combinations which increase their intensity and in balanced quantitative proportions.

Although stitching is not used directly as a colour element, it can intensify colour by creating texture. I use a free machine stitch and invisible nylon thread to give a random 'quilted' effect, which bonds the fabrics together and gives a unified surface.

'Lowestoft Beach' (which was commissioned for Norwich Castle Museum's Modern Art Collection) is the first piece that I completed after a year's sabbatical due to the birth of my son. This event had a strong influence on both the making and the content of the piece. The hand-painted fabrics and the emphasis on mark-making have been replaced by the plain, brightly coloured fabrics of earlier work and a return to greater figurative and pictorial depth. But most importantly, becoming a mother seems to have unlocked a greater humanity in my work. This is the first time in my fabric pieces that I have included figures. In fact, the canvas was so teeming with life that I had to remove some of the bodies to make the composition work.

Thomas also brought a flood of bright colour into my life in the form of toys. Although I had wanted to use these 'synthetic' colours ever since moving to the coast, it wasn't until I'd spent a year surrounded by plastic toys that I was able to use them harmoniously in this piece. The key was in establishing the bright colour range first, and then working 'back to front', using the bright colours as a foil for the more subtle ones. Finally, the tiny highlights of fluorescent colour – the plastic seaside ephemera – were added to form an abstract pattern leading the eye round the canvas as it zigzags with the figures into the distance.

At the time, however, the picture-making process is more instinctive and mysterious than this, and it is only afterwards that one can be more analytical about it.

# HELEN DANIEL

I MAKE EXCLUSIVELY hand-stitched pieces in a variety of sizes. Small pieces are up to 12 in (30 cm) square and the larger works, mainly for commission, are up to 80 × 40 in (2 × 1 m).

My work is of a personal nature, with an illustrative element. Ideas come from a myriad of sources, some deliberately sought and others which surprise me. They tend to be stored away in my subconscious for some time, remaining dormant until, with a burst of activity, several images are produced in series. Ideas evolve from special moments, relationships, travel, a love of gardens, invented stories and sometimes things which just strike me as being interesting or amusing.

Drawing is an important part of my working process. Working outside in sketchbooks is most stimulating, with the exploration of line, mark, colour and texture in mixed media such as watercolour, inks, pencil, crayon and pastels. Animals, foliage and landscape are fascinating subjects. Such sketchbook work is never directly translated into fabric but functions as an idea and thinking activity essential to the whole process.

*'Autumn Leaves', 1991. a. 11 × 8½ in (28 × 22 cm), b. 12½ × 8¼ in (31 × 21 cm),*
*c. 10¾ × 8½ in (27 × 22 cm). Cotton*
*This piece is part of a series of small embroideries which took the pavements of Manchester in*
*October, when they are covered in beautiful jewel-coloured leaves, as their influence*

*'Disco Dog and the Banana Patch'*, 1992. 42 × 24 in (107 × 61 cm). Cotton and silk
*'Disco Dog'* is about a dog called Bessie in Bermuda. She is a bit dizzy and the piece reflects
her personality

*'Telstar Mix', 1992. 17½ × 20½ in (44 × 52 cm). Cotton and silk*

'Telstar Mix', detail

*I visit friends in Bermuda on a regular basis and the island has become very influential in providing ideas and stories. This piece is about me constructing a rockery one day. Telstar Mix is a kind of bedding plant which I bought at the nursery*

I love to handle fabric and thread, using mainly cotton with some scraps of silk. I feel that a conventional table is constricting and so work on the floor, finding it comfortable to sit amongst piles of fabric, threads and beads. As a working method I tear, cut and assemble strips of fabric. A ground surface is made up from the strips and cut images are applied. The surface is then decorated with stitches, the process joining the separated elements to form one cloth. I use simple techniques and do not find it necessary to sample. However, recently seams, bindings and edges have been researched in order to extend my working processes. I enjoy basic stitches, investigating their mark-making capacities in a decorative manner. The application of beads has become an additional way of making marks and decorating surfaces. The construction of borders has evolved as an essential starting point, contributing structure and providing an image with an enclosure.

The fabric is dyed in colours which I find stimulating. Delight is found in the unexpected qualities produced. I react in a very positive way to strong colour, which has further developed from the influence of the dramatic colour and light values found in hot countries. The uninhibited use of colour in ethnic and folk embroidery is an additional influence. Colour harmonies and discords play an important role in the way I select fabric.

I aim to express optimism and a sense of joy in my work.

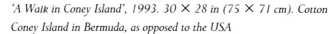

*'A Walk in Coney Island', 1993. 30 × 28 in (75 × 71 cm). Cotton*
*Coney Island in Bermuda, as opposed to the USA*

# SARAH DENISON

I AIM TO produce textiles of a very high quality. They should glow with warmth and humanity and be cherished family heirlooms.

The ideas behind my work are fairly simple. I don't feel the need to tackle large issues and tend to steer away from deep questions. Thus my approach to embroidery is visual and straightforward. Presently I treat it as a joyful, decorative art – something which brings great pleasure, something which makes people smile.

I really like working in series. I delight in rows of things all lined up, working together, interlinked – the more the merrier. A lone piece upsets me, and even two pieces worry me. Three or more and I'm happy.

*'The Pot', 1993. 93 × 100 in (236 × 254 cm), detail. Cornely and domestic machine embroidery on silk dupion*

*'The Pot', detail*

*'Cloth of Earthly Delights', 1992. 93 × 89 in (236 × 226 cm). Cornely and domestic
machine embroidery on silk dupion*

*'Cloth of Earthly Delights', detail. Cornely chain and mossing stitch*

The imagery is mainly influenced by those things I enjoy most in life: antiques, good cuisine, embroidery, ceramics, my pets, Italy and architecture. I don't go out specifically looking for ideas or inspiration. Once I have decided on a germ of a design, I will retrace my steps and seek out books, postcards, holiday snaps, anything which appeals to me, whether they are in museums, art galleries or a supermarket.

A great deal of time is spent amassing visual information. Usually there is more than enough, and careful editing reduces it all to a chosen few. I sketch, choose fabric and silks, make decisions. Eventually work begins in earnest, with plenty of room for possible readjustments. Thereafter the piece develops itself as it goes along. I will unpick and move things or take them out completely if I'm unhappy with them, even if they've taken days. Colours work or they don't, and stitches likewise; often it is not until I've done something that I know it's right or wrong.

The inspiration for my hanging 'Cloth of Earthly Delights' came from an exquisite little museum in York, the Museum of Automata. I was so thrilled by everything there – the miniature silk costumes, the engineering skills which went into making an eye wink, the bizarre subject matter of smoking moon dandies, juggling monkeys and acrobatic pigs. The piece virtually constructed itself, I was so swept away. Alongside toys I put my pot dogs, my collection of bottle corks and so on, until the whole was covered with favourite objects. Although I had not consciously intended it, the layout came to resemble that of an old cross-stitch sampler.

I work continuously, getting as much as possible done as quickly as possible, before the enthusiasm goes. Although the actual working of the embroidery is very mechanistic, I am lucky enough to have a Cornely sewing machine on which I can work, thoroughly engrossed, for hours.

# MARIA-THERESA FERNANDES

STITCHERY IS used as mark-marking or drawing in my work. Its various thicknesses and directions create texture, line, expression and movement. I make embroidery in conjunction with other media as in collage. In some cases it is used as line for expression. The surface can be fine handmade paper, which is ideal for machine embroidery. Thick handmade paper tends to clog the machine and, therefore, is not suitable for this kind of work. Free machine embroidery with the loop stitch is also used, and straight stitch in various directions will suggest movement.

Transparency is an effect I have been working with over the past two years. In 'Spiritual Encounters', the silk organdie is juxtaposed and overlapped to create illusion and color. Both hand and machine embroidery are used to give texture, tonality and line. Because light is important in this piece, the work is hung in mid-air so the light can penetrate the silk surfaces. The outer edges are circular, representing the continuity of life. The serpent represents the immortality of life. Dye pigments are painted on to give an overall effect and a cohesiveness to the composition. The circle is irregular, flexible and light. The wrapped threads in various colors on the outer frame are a unifying element of the work.

*'Spiritual Encounters', 1991. 72 × 36 × 1 in (183 × 91 × 2.5 cm). Silk, copper wire, paint and machine stitchery*
*The circle symbolizes the continuity in life, like the snake that sheds its skin and is reborn again*

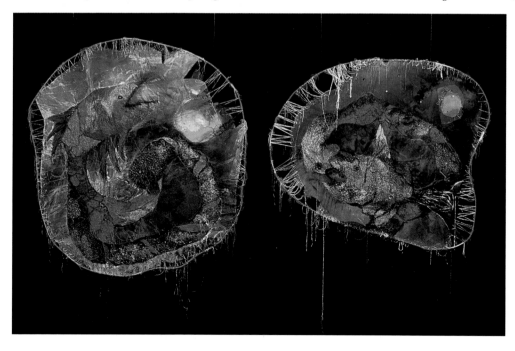

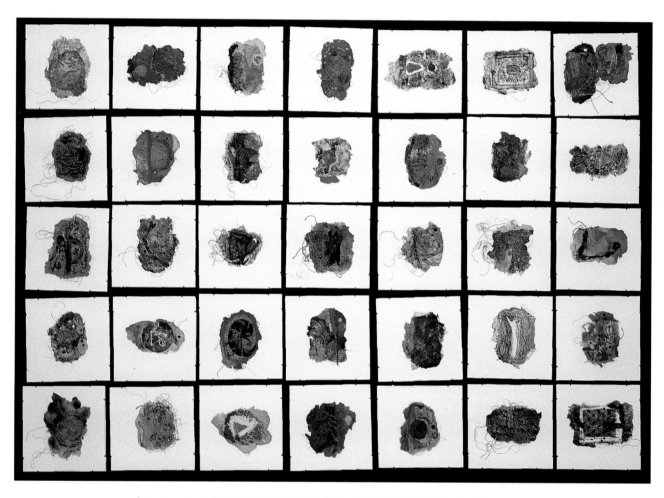

*'Egyptian Symbols', 1990. 60 × 72 × ¹⁄₄ in (152 × 183 × 0.6 cm). Mono-print, handmade paper, hand and machine embroidery*

All the works illustrated here relate to my trip to Egypt. I found that being there both stimulated and fascinated me. The symbols are universal and personal. The individual units are made of fine copper wire. The pieces are intimate and portray various stories. The mark-marking is spontaneous and stitchery is used as drawing in conjunction with mono-printing and collage. The background is silk organdie and is interlaced freely onto the flexible copper frame. The colors are bright and vibrant, relating to the colors of Egypt and my own African birthplace.

Since moving to the USA ten years ago, the cultural diversity and the music, particularly jazz, have been a stimulus for my work. Art is my life; the two are inseparable. Most of my time is spent in my studio, which is part of an old school. I like complexities and enjoy working on several pieces simultaneously. My work is an ongoing process and it is difficult to gauge the time spent on individual pieces.

*'Pyramid V', 1990. 24 × 24 × 12 in (61 × 61 × 30 cm). Silk, paint, hand and machine embroidery*

# LISSY FUNK

I DISCOVERED THE art of textiles at the age of eighteen, after having trained as a dancer. As captivating as dance was for me, I could not see my future in it. Drawing and painting were too fast for me. I needed something that would grow from within, that I could create slowly, at my own pace. So I took up needle and thread, and embroidered two blue-and-white panels. The needle moved across the cloth, which sometimes seemed endless. I was gripped with excitement by the possibilities that needlework offers for artistic self-expression. The technique presented me with a rich and limitless world. I knew it was for me. I became an embroiderer and worked day and night.

*'Red, White and Blue', 1989. 13¾ × 11¾ in (35 × 30 cm)*

*'White', 1989. 15¾ × 11¾ in (40 × 30 cm)*

The process of creation is long and tedious. I must never give up on the concept that I see in my mind's eye; I must be willing to start over again and again, sometimes without hope of success. Often when I think that everything is totally lost, the wall-hanging begins to walk, showing me the way. The feeling is wonderful. It is true happiness. We live together and everything is fine.

What do I try to say in my needlework? This is difficult to express, because words can destroy a delicate concept that is still coming into being. So much flows together from so many different directions: experience, desires and knowledge of many kinds. In the end, the embroidery carries all of these elements in itself. From the wall it looks at you, in order to reach you, to strike up a conversation, and, if you are willing, to accompany you and stay with you.

The fabrics and threads are natural materials, such as linen, cotton, wool and silk. While a piece is being executed, it is attached to a beam suspended from the ceiling which can easily be raised or lowered. The needlework is done in circular sections in fabric that is tightly stretched in a round hoop held in place by a leather belt. Large expanses of fabric are layered with coloured yarns by using an extensive vocabulary comprising up to fifty traditional stitches. Vast areas are worked in the Funk Stitch: this couching holds unprocessed, unspun wool or flax in place from the reverse.

The small and crowded studio is an active place. To do large pieces a number of assistants are employed. Generally it takes fourteen to seventeen hours to embroider 1 square in (6.45 square cm). Larger pieces require many months, and sometimes years, to make.

Work goes on on several pieces at the same time. If an area does not please, hours of work are undone within minutes. There is no specific reason for using a particular stitch – the choice is based on a search that begins before its application . . . If any stitches need to be removed because they turn out to feel wrong, they are simply removed. This is a daily occurrence. In the end, the wall-hangings themselves demand and dictate their specific needs. It is only through a continuous dialogue between the work and me that the selection of stitches and other decisions are made. Only by living with the hangings for extended periods and working on them several times a day do I know when a piece is completed.

# NICOLE GAULIER

ONE DAY in 1980, I decided to conduct a trial of strength with the chain stitch. It would be a case of who had the last word. From that time, I have tried to uncover all the secrets of this ordinary little stitch . . . up to now I have had the last word. Instead of being exhausted, I become more and more excited by all the artistic possibilities of embroidery.

My initial work is in oil pastels. I draw with speed and spontaneity to achieve movement, colour, light and an element of surprise. I cut up my pastel drawings and the embroideries develop from these. The embroideries are made more slowly in lines of chain stitch, and these lines are worked in three, two or one strand of DMC cotton. The play of light, creating tonal effects on the threads, is an important part of my stitching.

When the embroidery is finished it is washed and ironed. This process means the piece usually alters, the surface is distorted a little; I see this as part of the finished textile.

My embroidery is miniature – 4 × 4 in (10 × 10 cm) – which means I challenge myself to concentrate the idea and pinpoint the essential. I do not have any particular message; I enjoy making formal compositions with abstract shapes. My embroideries are a form of handwriting.

*Broderie, detail*

*Broderie, 1988. 6¾ × 5 in (17 × 13 cm). Cotton, chain stitch*

# PAM GAUNT

MY WORK addresses autobiographical concerns to do with various relationships and experiences. While the subject matter is personal, much of the way I work stems from my interest in old cloth, heavily embroidered and ornate textiles from the past, aerial views of landscape and my desire to merge these influences with contemporary imagery and use of materials. Thus my work is always experimental in terms of its inclusion of non-traditional materials – wood, foil, books, memorabilia, broken needles. Basically I include anything that can be stitched/glued into the work where appropriate.

*'Threads of Journeys', detail*

*'Threads of Journeys', 1991. 49 × 38 in (125 × 97 cm). Small-scale quilt. Silks, cottons, vanishing muslin, dyed balsa wood, broken needles, foils, stamps and plastic. Hand and machine embroidery*
*As the title suggests, the piece continues to address my interest in meaning and memory through the physical layering of materials and visual ambiguities*

*'Thoughts, Words and Things', 1989. 50 × 56 in (127 × 143 cm)*
*Conceived some years after my mother's death, this work explores notions of personal and collective*
*memories through the visual interplay of surface and depth, visibility and invisibility*

My recent work contains 'threads' from past pieces, but more specifically addresses the notion of meaning and memory: the change in the meaning of objects after the death of the owner, or a relationship, and how new meaning evolves. This was initially triggered by my mother's death in 1977, when I was left with numerous objects to sort through, some of which were significant and became even more so, and others which left me in a dilemma.

Another important aspect of my work is the nature of construction and layering. This has always been part of the way I have worked. As well as being layered, the works are generally constructed, deconstructed and reconstructed, achieving the final appearance through no other process. The layering is both physical and metaphorical in that it conceals and reveals areas, adding an element of mystery or secrecy to the work. Layering is also a physical means of achieving the illusion of depth with colour in more ethereal work, the latter two aspects being a source of constant fascination to me.

Drawing is usually done parallel to samples. The nature of the work, being heavily layered in parts, makes it difficult to draw; therefore drawings tend to be about structure and tone, and are often collaged.

Textiles, and all they embrace, are the essence of my work. I constantly refer to tradition through the various processes or material inclusions. One of my aims is to expose the traditional processes of making textiles that have been hidden in the past, and integrate them into my work. I like to use elements such as raw edges, seams, tacking, loose threads, broken needles, and expose their inherent aesthetic qualities as part of the work.

This approach allows my work to make constant reference to tradition but also to deal simultaneously with personal and contemporary issues and imagery.

# NICOLA HENLEY

OVER THE past two years, trips to Gambia, Nepal, India, Australia and Japan have been great sources of inspiration. Traditional textile techniques, such as stitch-resist dyed indigo and Aboriginal rock and bark painting, as well as new imagery, texture and colour, have all been influential in the development of my work. My ornithological inspiration, however, remains essentially fired by birds of the British Isles.

I place great emphasis on studying birds in the field, because it allows me to develop new ways of drawing and recording moving birds, as well as giving an opportunity to absorb the environment. This is essential in order to create a lively, impressionistic piece of work. It is also a healthy contrast to the close, long hours spent working in the studio. Currently I work in a converted stone barn, near the shores of Lough Derg, set in the heart of the hills of County Clare, western Ireland. The countryside, colours and birds provide a constant source of inspiration.

*'Cormorant Movement', 1990. 25½ × 27 in (65 × 68 cm), detail*

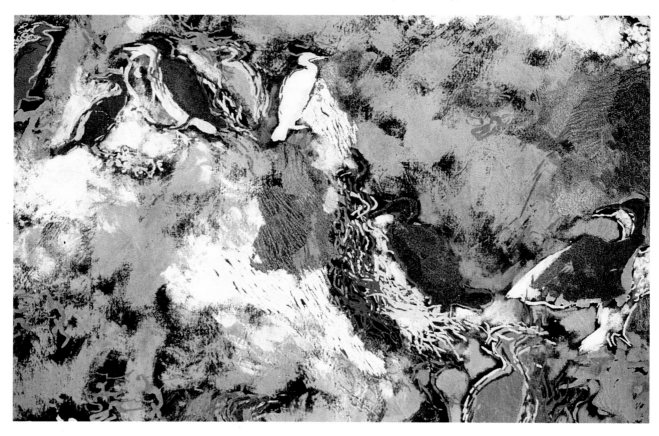

68

'Oystercatchers, Valencia, Eire', 1992. 69 × 36½ in (175 × 93 cm). Dyed calico, screen-printed and painted with discharge pigments; applied muslin, lace and paper. Machine and hand embroidery

This piece was composed from a series of sketches of the wader feeding with its characteristic rapid, searching movements amongst the weeds and shells of the Valencia Island shores, off County Kerry

'Crow Descent',
1990.
38 × 24½ in
(96 × 62 cm)

*'Cattle Egrets',*
*1990.*
*32 × 49 in*
*(82 × 125 cm),*
*detail*

My embroidery is used either to embellish the surface, creating a textural richness often seen only when the viewer is close to the work, or as a strong contrast to the printed surface. For example, slightly drawn-up running stitch can create an area of tension in the fabric, suggesting movement. Free machining is worked on to the printed surface, sometimes holding down a variety of materials, such as threads, paper, silk or previously printed fine cloth.

I value more and more the freedom from the restraints which might arise if I tried to keep to one discipline. To be able to paint directly on to cloth, as well as being able to use a range of hand and machine embroidery techniques, affords me a great deal of freedom and flexibility. I try to capture the sense of space and pattern of movement of birds within their environment, constantly inspired by their unique freedom as well as by each bird's characteristics. I am interested in the idea of space contrasting with close detail, as I see when observing birds in their habitats. The key elements of flight patterns and typical settings are sometimes conveyed by symbolic marks, as on a map. Sometimes bird's-eye views are incorporated, helped occasionally by drawing from a balloon.

# AGNETA HOBIN

The difference between living in the town and living in the countryside is one of the basic things in my life as an artist. When staying at our log cabin in eastern Finland, where life is very simple, very close to nature, I feel that values return to their right proportions.

The origins of my themes as an artist lie in the lake landscape of Puruvesi. My works arise out of quintessentially Finnish horizons between land and water, light and darkness, winter and summer – frontiers characterized by the near abstract, subtly shifting nuances of ice, snow, water, air, light. I try to find counterparts for them in my materials in motion, structure, traces, images and memory. My darker works contain extreme states contrasted with the light – the subtle refraction of deep hues like black; the dark, heavy slumber of the earth.

*'Navigare Dolce', II, 1986. 8 × 14 × 2⅔ in (20 × 36 × 7 cm). Embroidered piece, pure silk. A piece of wood fits inside; this allows the work to stand*

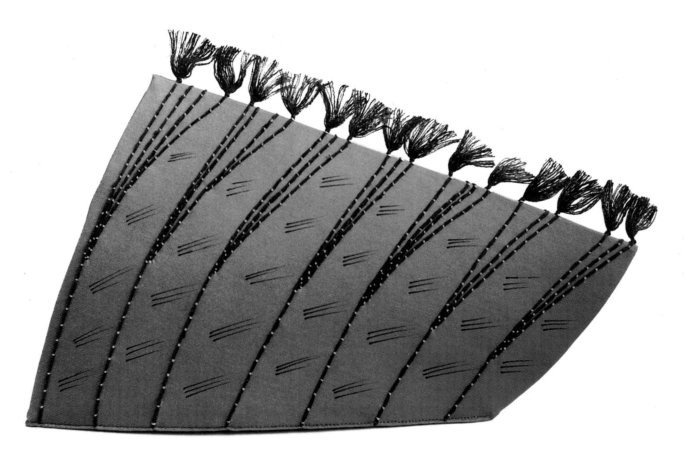

*'Navigare Dolce', 1990. 8 × 14 × 2⅔ in (20 × 36 × 7 cm). Embroidered piece, pure silk.*
*A piece of wood fits inside; this allows the work to stand*

First, I have an idea or theme that I want to express, and then I start examining ways I might do this. Mostly, I use drawing and painting, and also photography to some extent. I think it is very important to see the actual size and proportions of the piece at an early stage, so I make 1:1 sketches on paper. I am not attached to any special technique; as a textile artist I want to be free. Often my pieces are made by others. I believe in joint work: when an artist and a craftsman join in a process, I think together they can achieve good results.

Some of my themes and goals decide my way of proceeding. I see my work as a whole, so I don't belittle any part of it, be it idea, technique, material, realization or finally mounting and exhibiting of the piece.

'Navigare Dolce' is a three-dimensional piece standing on a 'foot' of wood, which is placed into the embroidered silk-piece from the opening at the bottom. The surface of the form is silk, sewn on to a stiff, thick slab of plastic foam. The decoration of the form is made in pure silk; the silk threads are placed on the material as long stripes and then attached to the material by small stitches, which at the same time form a kind of decoration as small pearl-like white dots.

The 'Navigare' theme has its origin in the forms of the tail and fin of the salmon. I worked a great deal on this theme, experimenting with different materials and sizes. The dots and stripes on the surface of the forms resemble those on the salmon. I have used the pure silk thread in a simple way, attaching the loose threads on the material with the small dots of silk. I have no ambition to use stitches in an orthodox manner, doing it 'right'. No, I want only to express something. In this case it is the salmon – its shape, the ornamental dots and stripes, and its colour. And I want to do things my own way, so it's not meant to be a photograph but an impression.

# Lillevi Hultman

WHEN I WAS a small girl, my grandfather gave me a toy sewing machine. The stitches it made were not the best and often the result was a complete mess. I lost interest and forgot my sewing machine until I was in my last year at the National College of Art and Design. Then I found the method of expression that had always been with me; machine embroidery became a new means of communication.

Over the years I have made work in a variety of sizes. My embroideries vary from small to large – 119 × 159½ in (3 × 4 m). I moved to a large scale when collaborating with the Association of Friends of Textile Art (an institute where they sew and weave from plans produced by artists). Earlier I had often worked directly with the sewing machine or used a draft, but now I make accurate plans for the work.

*'Gate', 1989. 18½ × 20½ in (47 × 52 cm). Machine embroidery*

*'She', 1988. 7¾ × 11 in (20 × 28 cm). Machine embroidery*
*This hanging is in a hospital waiting-room for female patients*

'The Mapping, or Homage to Barbro Sandin', 1990. 15¼ × 12½ in (39 × 32 cm).
Appliqué on cotton. Machine embroidery
This work is a homage to a famous therapist in Sweden

I work in my studio at home, and sometimes I collaborate with the Association of Friends of Textile Art in Stockholm. 'The Mapping, or Homage to Barbro Sandin' is an embroidery produced from such a collaboration. The embroidered pieces are covered with linen threads and applied to a painted cotton fabric. The work was made for the Psychology Institute at the University of Linköping, where it now hangs. In it I am mapping the essential human 'self' (the triangle in the middle) and what we encounter in life (the forms around).

I embroider abstract forms with known symbols. External influences come from other arts and from fragments of my own surroundings. Coloured surfaces have become the major part of my work. Sometimes I fill in the surface with several layers of threads or thread bunches (made of cut pieces of sewing thread). In this way I cover a dark surface with a lighter one, so that dark patches are seen here and there. Sometimes I add another motif on the previously embroidered surface. On large pieces I start by applying embroidered surfaces to a painted or stained background.

# JAN IRVINE

I N SUBJECT matter, my work is generally atmospheric, using landscape as a base and developing symbols and significance from light and movement within it. As an expression of self, my images have a personal meaning, but they can also be interpreted freely as purely decorative or with varying levels of meaning.

Ten years ago, when I was teaching fabric skills in the Australian desert, I found I had visual images pressing for expression. It was a natural step to use textiles as my means of expression, and I began by piecing symbolic landscapes.

I moved through a progression of groupings of tonal colours to overlaying chiffons until I found airbrush dyeing to satisfy my search for subtlety of shape and colour in my compositions. I find the gentle colour of dye to fabric afforded by airbrushing allows me to merge colours more subtly and with a more pleasing working style than other dyeing methods.

*'Animate', 1990. 43 × 63 in (111 × 160 cm). Airbrushed dyed raw silk, wool filled, hand stitched*
*I have used a stem stitch to create a continuous line in the composition in addition to the usual quilters' running stitch. The composition refers to the intangible energies and influences at work in our world*

*'Juxtaposed', 1990. 39 × 47 in (100 × 120 cm). Airbrushed dyed raw silk, wool filled, hand stitched*

*The image in this work (one in the same series as 'Animate') shows the juxtaposition of opposites, using the example of static and active*

I've used a variety of fabrics for their different effects. Cottons give a gentler, aged appearance and silks retain a rich dye colour. Wool or cotton wadding fills the work and threads vary from fine sewing thread to industrial thread for larger work.

My stitching develops the visual concepts. I draw on both quilting and embroidery traditions, but rather than having grown from technique, technique has followed the dictate of the visual purpose. I use the thread as line, with stitching as a graphic mark. The close rows of running stitch draw the surface together with something of the charm of antique quilts. The visual depth this adds to the airbrushed cloth is from particles of light bouncing in all directions off the ruckled face of the work.

I produce textiles on full and miniature scale. The small works are generally more thoroughly stitched for intimate viewing, while the larger works use colour and broader stitching for impact at a greater distance.

*'Aerodrome', 1987. 71 × 102 in (180 × 260 cm). Airbrushed dyed raw silk, wool filled, hand stitched*
*This composition comments on the integrity of tribal values in Australia*

# LOUISE JAMET

My INTEREST in sewing and embroidery, and for fibres in general, is the result of many circumstances. As a child, play was often associated with fabric, as I used left-over materials from my mother's sewing to make costumes for myself, or clothes for my dolls or my cats. Later on, during my formal training as an artist in the 1970s, renewed interest in fibre techniques as an art medium was brought about partly by modernism, which encouraged the exploration of a wide range of media and materials, and partly by the feminist movement, which tried to reassert and bring in to the public sphere women's activities, long related to the home and devalued.

*'Kuujjuarrpik: The Rock', 1991. 15 × 22 in (38 × 55 cm). Hand and machine embroidery, photocopy transfers on cotton, bamboo, muslin, paint, stone*

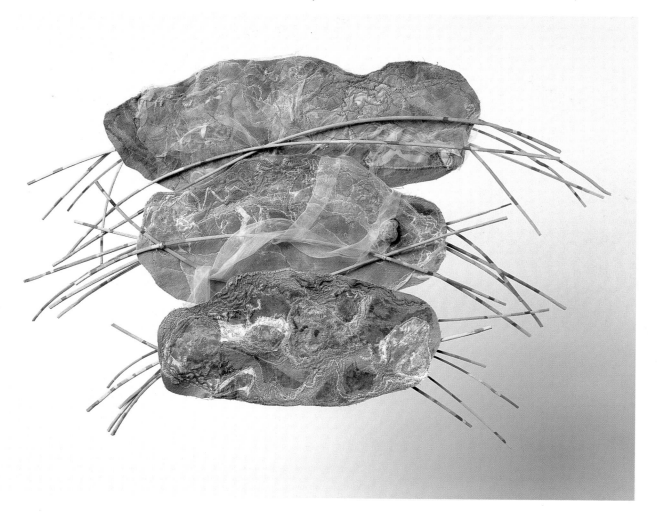

'Blue Jay', 1989. 23 × 16½ in (58 × 42 cm). Hand and machine embroidery, photocopy transfers, fabric dyeing (**shibori**), bamboo and feathers

*'Blue Jay'*, detail

Sewing and embroidery have been associated with domestic work and the leisure time of women. My early exploration involved going beyond the restrictions of practical use and decoration, and searching for their specificity through a modernist, self-referential approach. It also involved investigating the historical, ethnological and sociological aspects of these media, as well as the particular vocabulary, materials and techniques, to point out the process and to extend their formal possibilities. I tried to rediscover the essence of sewing and embroidery which had been concealed or forgotten through their development and their use for utilitarian purposes or decoration. The work resulting from this investigation displayed the characteristics of fibre: flexibility and continuity.

I usually work in series. In early explorations, sewing and embroidery were medium and subject all at once, and inspiration was drawn from samplers, quilts, sewing baskets and sewing materials. The stitches were kept basic and simple – running stitch, seed stitch and variations on satin stitch – while colour·photocopies were often cut up beyond recognition and used as small, colourful shapes, much like in a collage or as a pattern. The elements were limited and kept simple voluntarily to show the process.

More recently, having moved from the city to the country, my perception has been greatly stimulated by the new shapes and textures present in my natural environment – animal tracks, the black-and-white patterns of Holstein cows, mosses and lichens, farm buildings and signs. My present work is inspired initially in its formal aspect by medieval banners and pennants, and could be described as autobiographical. These little 'flags' are personal emblems and as a series they could be seen as pages of a journal which records moments in time. The subjects, mostly animals or birds, symbolize stages of the personal evolution brought about by my transition from the city to the country. The slower pace and more pragmatic reality of rural life promote introspection, and this series marks specific experiences of this journey.

Technically, the work combines hand and machine embroidery, sewing, fabric dyeing, photocopy transfers and bamboo sticks, which have a structural function as they define the shape of the 'flags'. These sticks are often coloured with pencils or paint to show bands of geometric pattern which provide a link with the fabric part of the work. Each 'flag' differs greatly from the others and each one is elaborated as a separate entity to convey its own meaning.

Although I use various techniques and elements to translate my concepts into material objects, sewing and embroidery are always central to my work as they represent a celebration of women's work and indulge my personal affinity with fibre.

# WALTRAUD JANZEN

USUALLY MY embroidered pictures and objects develop during the process of creation. No drawings are made, no sketches are used. The idea behind my work is to create pictures and objects, well-balanced colour and composition. I often use 'useless', discarded things in my work, in combination with embroidery and precious material like silk, to show their hidden beauty, hoping that people will become aware of their environment.

Arranging small patches of colour and structure and the slow process of embroidering are like music to me. Therefore, many of the titles of my pictures are taken from the field of music – for example, 'Capriccio'.

I prefer to use appliqué techniques and machine embroidery in my work. Textile materials in their great variety give me inspiration. The size of most of my pieces is fairly small, because embroidered pictures require close contact with the viewer.

*'Secret Message', 1989. 7½ × 7½ in (19 × 19 cm). Silk on canvas, appliqué, with machine embroidery*

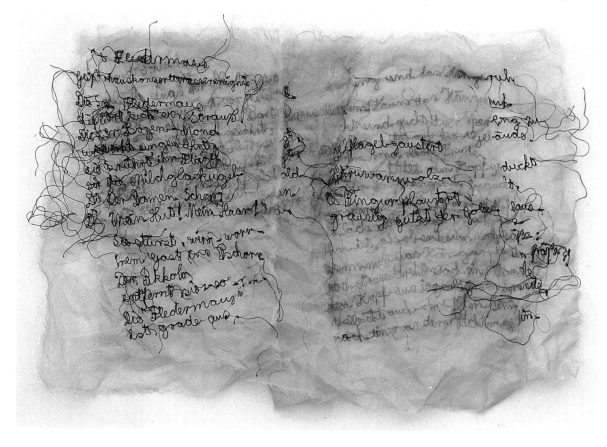

'Capriccio', 1990. 12 × 8 in (30 × 20 cm). Different threads on silk and canvas, appliqué,
with machine and hand embroidery

I like to work with transparent materials which show a very delicate quality of colour, especially if they are put together in layers of different thickness. I love tender colours and modify their appearance by shades of overlaid embroidery. I also love to use stitching as a graphic means: I 'draw' or 'write' with the needle. I therefore often cover the whole work with needle-writing.

Since no sketches are used for my abstract pictures, I see the artwork through its development. It is always very exciting for me to 'feel' what the material wants, so I let the embroidery grow. Sometimes I pad the background or parts of it, hence the embroidery looks quilted. In this case, I use colour very cautiously and sparingly. I work on several pictures at a time; this gives me the chance to put the work aside and to look at it from a distance in time and space to examine it again and again.

'Bowl', 1990. 4 × 5 in (10 × 13 cm) diameter. Very small pieces of translucent silk are sewn by hand into an irregular mini-patchwork, which is shaped like a bowl

# ALICE KETTLE

$M$Y EMBROIDERY is an extension of painting, which I studied and worked at before I took up embroidery. When I made the change I was aware that the two activities are closely related, but embroidery was a medium which helped me to express my individuality. We have grown up together.

I approach work on each embroidery in the same way as painting, seeking to make a satisfactory piece of art, a balanced composition using line and colour. Then the making takes over – a very important feature that draws me to this particular textile.

*'Indian Summer Man', detail*

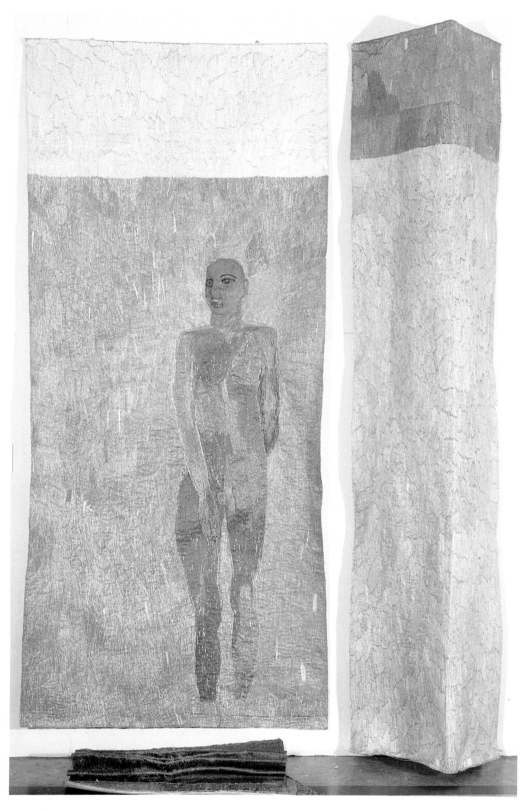

'Indian Summer Man', 1990. The central figure is 125 × 47 in (320 × 120 cm)
The figure emerges from a background which contains shimmering, oblique light. Man embodies a
state of calmness; he is any man, even any woman

'Creation', 1990–91. 144 × 96 in (366 × 244 cm). Stitched textile: silk, metal, cotton
thread
The work was inspired by a visit to India. It represents the poised spirit of the people, the powerful
shimmering light

There is always a figure in my work. That's because it is essentially about myself. A piece might be about my reaction to a place, a poem, a painting, a person. For example, 'Creation' was inspired by the golden, contemplative quality of the light in India, where I had travelled in order to visit their textile centres. Even a thought or a mood can inspire a piece. The larger hangings, because of their imposing size, tend to be of upright, classical poses. These take months to complete and may be a series of several hangings; they are the scale I feel most at home with. The smaller pieces break into more relief on their surfaces. They are about movement, stretching, writhing and floating figures.

The technique is intensive machine embroidery. The threads entirely cover whatever base material I use, often in several layers. The technique produces folds. Areas which I want particularly to mould are stitched over and over until they are hard and stand out from the surface. I use several threads at one time, changing the tension continuously so that they mix together in different ways.

The threads are any I can find: all thicknesses and types of silk, cotton, rayon and metal. They all respond differently to light, to create extraordinary nuances of colour. A piece can develop from one thread.

I don't really plan work, although looking back I can trace a logical evolution over several years; each piece springs from the previous one. The figure grows as I work, and tremendous changes can take place. I once saw a film of Matisse painting a picture and changing it dramatically ten times. I work in much the same way. Obviously, for commission the work is more tightly planned, with preliminary drawings and samples, but again in the working of the piece subtleties develop in an intuitive way.

I sometimes wonder why I work in embroidery. It is so slow. You may ruthlessly have to discard several weeks' work as it becomes clear that it is unsatisfactory. But I feel as though I am unwrapping a parcel and discovering more and more. This excitement is what keeps me going on.

# SUSANNE KLINKE

A LL MY work is developed around the theme of the human figure. There is not a clear-cut message, but rather different contexts for the figure allow for a variety of possible interpretations. I work in a number of sizes, depending on the materials and techniques I am using in any given piece.

My working method is to use a very spontaneous approach to the development of an idea. I do not draw or design a piece before starting. Often the materials are the inspiration to begin; it is inspiration through textiles.

*'Still Gelegt', detail*

*'Still Gelegt', 1991. Two pieces together 55 × 55 × 27½ in (140 × 140 × 70 cm).*
*Zigzag machine embroidery on webbing combined with wood*

'Figure Band', 1987. 7½ × 7½ × 1¼ in (19 × 19 × 3 cm). Zigzag machine embroidery on webbing

Mostly I use old and second-hand materials, which are interesting to me because of their particular tactile quality. I try different techniques, but mostly use conventional hand and machine marks, which give a graphic structure to the work. The stitches I use are zigzag on the machine and satin stitch, back stitch, stem stitch and long and short stitch with hand embroidery.

This means that the contrast between light and dark is an important element, and I reject what are for me loud colours, as they would not aid my visual ideas.

*'Cut', 1990. 20½ × 32¼ in (52 × 82 cm). Zigzag machine embroidery on webbing*

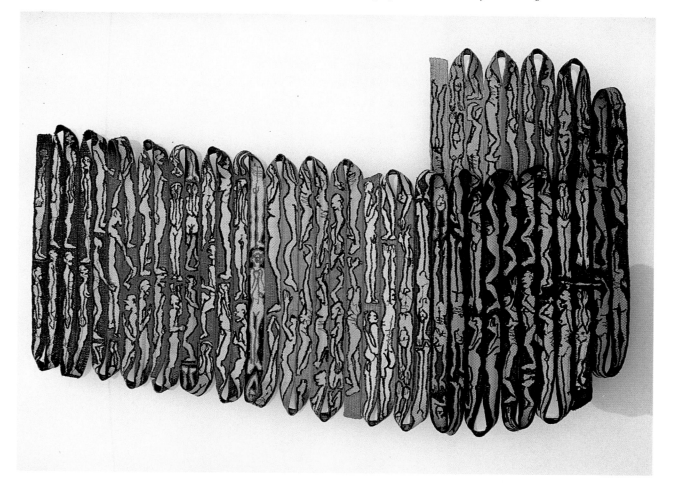

# JANET LEDSHAM

SINCE MOVING to Ireland in 1972, the main inspiration for my work has been my personal perception of the surrounding landscape. Recurring themes are the marshland and moorland bogs of County Antrim and Donegal, and the distinctive topographic features associated with these habitats. Small-scale stitched sketches executed on location provide the initial sources of reference. I also record environmental images photographically, and these provide me with the basic information for pieces of a more experimental nature. My aim is to create an authentic interpretation through the medium of textiles which will evoke memories that are associated with a particular time and place.

*'Sunshine and Shadows', 1989. 54 × 54 in (137 × 137 cm), detail. Handmade felt, incorporating natural materials and personal correspondence, quilted with hand and machine stitching*
*Sunshine and shadows refer to the patchwork technique. I have exploited the tendency to use personal letters as templates to save expense, the fragmented words giving clues about the maker*

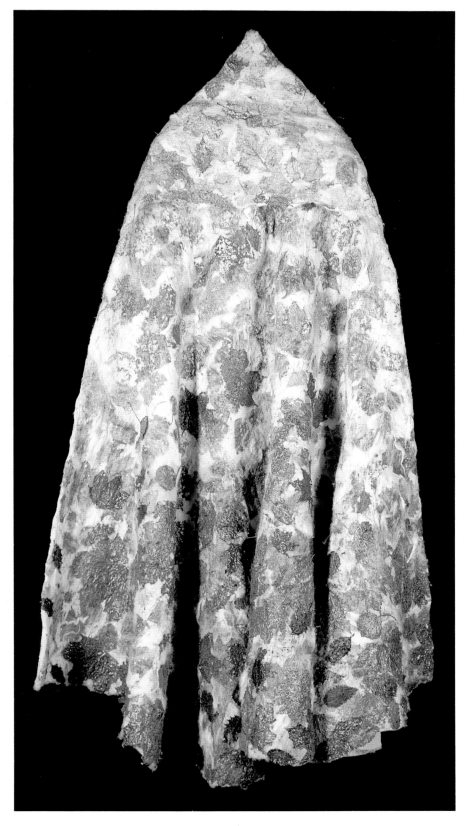

*'Mary's Mantle', 1991. 63 × 55 in (160 × 140 cm). Handmade felt, incorporating leaves, quilted with machine stitching*

Since 1984, I have been making felt. Incorporated into the substrate are natural materials which have been collected on location. There is such variability in the sizes and shapes of the material, which range from the small, delicate seed-heads of thistles to the largest maple leaves. With such a wealth of materials, I can create many patterns. The different textures and the wide range of subtle colours add richness to the felt surface. Free machining and hand stitching are used as further embellishment and also serve to quilt and attach the materials.

The materials I use in my work are fragile. This raises the question of its permanence, but I don't have any long-term answers regarding its durability, except to say that, after ten years of working with these materials, the individual pieces to date are still surprisingly robust. The only deterioration is perhaps in colour quality, and this is part of the natural process and is fundamental to the principles of my work.

I prefer to work on as large a scale as possible, because this allows for more opportunity to be expressive with my particular imagery. Longer development time for large pieces of work also allows for ongoing influences to be absorbed into the composition as the work proceeds.

Many sources of reference have influenced my work. I have been drawn by the similarity of some patchwork designs to those I have observed in the field patterns in County Antrim. My study of Irish patchwork quilts since the nineteenth century revealed that, to save expense, the quiltmakers used personal letters as templates. I have borrowed this idea and used it to develop the basic configurations on which the principles of patchwork are grounded, to create a personal translation.

Another source is the mantle or *kepenck* made and worn by the shepherds in Afghanistan and Turkey. The shape is also reminiscent of the hooded cloak which was worn extensively in Ireland until the eighteenth century. 'Mary's Mantle' forms a very personal tribute to my mother, who died while the work was in progress. Maple, holly and aspen leaves are incorporated into the felt. The materials are quilted together with machine stitching.

# TOM LUNDBERG

I USE ELEMENTS of the visual world to illuminate the experiences of the inner world on pieces of cloth.

Everyday life is the starting point for the objects that I make. They are time-markers, grounded in particular locations and momentary light conditions. These pictures are sparked by things I see, but they are not exact diary entries. Rather, my work is like a story or a dream, where images pulled from the stream of events are isolated and given a new life. These pictures use small details and glimpses of life to reflect larger cycles and the bigger, mysterious world.

The central pictures in my work are executed with needle and thread. I like embroidery's intimate connection with memory and domestic life and its history of story-telling. Even simple mending documents a moment and a need. Thread provides a line of color, while the needle offers precision, focus and direction. I use cotton, silk and metallic threads with long and short stitch and couching. During the slow, digestive ritual of creating, threads merge and become textures – surfaces which correspond to intensified states of mind.

*'Blue Buckle', 1990. 2 × 6 in (5 × 15 cm). Silk and metal threads on wool*
*A study of opposites: dark and light, opening and closing*

*'Hot Water', 1991. 8 × 8 in (20 × 20 cm). Long and short stitch with couching, cotton, silk and metallic threads*
*This is a study on inside and outside motifs found in everyday surroundings*

*'Thirst', 1990. 24 × 18 in (61 × 46 cm). Painted wood and embroidery on wool*
*This was made when I was ready to move from a house where I had lived long enough to put down*
*roots. The frame is inspired by medieval reliquaries – the way reliquaries contain a small object*
*within a larger narrative framework*

I admire the beauty of ritual textiles – fabrics which use the materials of the physical world to convey the world of the spirit. The embroidered emblems worn by priests and warriors have taught me how color and symbols can exist within richly textured surfaces. An embroidered badge is like a tattoo needle onto skin. Both signify initiation and rites of passage, and both share an initial impulse to mark the life that is being lived.

The pieces are conceived and executed on a small scale, which gives them a decorative and jewel-like quality. The imagery is of an intensive personal nature and at the same time the symbols are universal. The juxtaposition of the symbols gives the work a narrative quality with many unanswered questions, and this invites the viewer to want to know more and keep coming back to look again.

*'Thirst', detail*

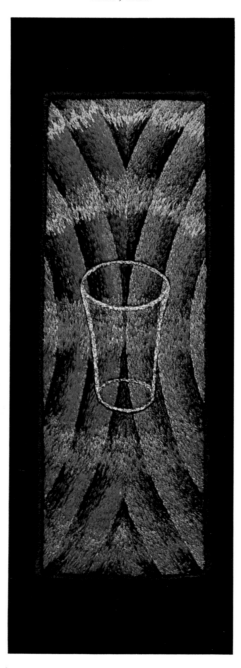

# Jane McKeating

THE IMAGERY for my textiles begins with drawings of my immediate environment. My images often focus on a moment, a fragment of time, that may have gone unnoticed and yet within it is a vast amount of colour, rhythm, poetry and energy.

*'Sewing down Spots', 1990. 19 × 30 in (48 × 76 cm). Hand and machine embroidery and print pigments on cotton*

*'Wiping the Table', 1991. 27 × 18 in (69 × 46 cm). Hand and machine stitching, procion dyes and print pigments*

I draw constantly, at every opportunity amidst the order and chaos within my domestic surroundings. 'Wiping the Table' was made when the only place I had to work was my dining-room table, which the family also had to eat at. The constant feeling of wiping away the clutter and mess, attempting to make space, was what I wanted to portray; to make room not only to work, but just to create some space. The cloth acts as a division between areas, and I have tried to use the stitch to convey the layers of muddle. I wanted it to feel as though the cloth was almost wiping the pattern off the table-cloth.

I find it is often a series of these drawings of a particular aspect of life that inspires me to make a new textile piece. I like to take an object and use it as a focal point. What happens to it moves a long way from the original drawings. The pieces are in one sense very illustrative of the stage of life I am currently at, and yet all have a common thread linking them that strives to express something deeper-rooted than at first appears. An instinctive sense of pattern-making, repeat and rhythm surfaces within each one, and this will often take over the work so that the starting point – the objective – in some senses appears incidental, even

*'Wiping the Table', detail*

though it is vitally important to me as a recognizable figure.

I am fascinated by this meeting point of the observed and recognizable, and the much more abstract areas of pattern-making, which for me express dance-like qualities. The nature of the stitch manages to link these areas together, creating one image. The resulting embroideries frequently have an energy and humour, as though the object has a life of its own.

My textiles are pieced together from various weights of cotton fabrics. These are dyed, bleached, painted and printed, sometimes before stitching, sometimes after and frequently both.

I work some areas with machine stitching on the Irish and domestic machine, and also increasingly work with hand stitching, finding that the combination gives the range of surfaces I enjoy so much when I draw.

Techniques are variable, but the work remains essentially flat. I respond to the fabric and figurative detail as I go along, using the machine needle rather as I would a pen or paintbrush. I love the instant colour-mixing that can transform the dyed surface by using many threads together or using a variety of techniques in combination. I love the change of pace between different techniques and use different ones to suit my state of mind, ranging from fast machining or enormous brushstrokes of dye to detailed hand stitch pattern-making. No piece relies on one method.

I rarely decide on the boundaries of a piece at the outset, preferring to arrive naturally at its edge when it instinctively 'feels right'. Usually fabric gets added and subtracted many times before a piece is concluded and is more frequently not 'squared off' in current work, as this often gives a formality not helpful to the imagery.

I work on a range of sizes from as small as 6 in (15 cm) up to 119 in (3 m), preferring somewhere in between, and I find my methods adapt to either scale.

I work in my dining room at home and my textiles are an extension and expression of my daily life. They work at their best when seen either within the context of a domestic interior or as a group, enabling them to respond to each other.

# ANNE McKENZIE NICKOLSON

M Y WORK is a vehicle for dealing with ideas, both visual and conceptual, that are of interest to me. Each piece represents a different prioritization of various ingredients – historic textiles, architecture, painting, nature and life experiences – all of which are combined, processed and reappear in new forms.

*'Aurora Borealis', 1990. 43 × 49 in (109 × 124 cm), detail. Immersion dyeing with procion dye, airbrush with textile pigments, hand embroidery on cotton. Mounted on stretched cotton fabric*

Pattern is a basic visual structure in my pieces. It can be as simple as a series of stripes, energetic zigzag lines or more elaborate pattern units derived from exotic plants and animals. Historic textiles frequently geometricize organic forms in order to rectify them with the grid of the fabric. As a surface designer, I can choose either an organic or a geometric presentation of a motif, and enjoy using both forms. Pattern units that have been so abstracted that they resemble both plants and animals are of special interest to me. Architecture, as evidenced in my own home, houses in my neighborhood and in my travels, which exhibits qualities of the human touch – arched doorways and

windows, trellises, leaded-glass windows, tilework, brickwork, weathervanes – has frequently entered my textiles. The subtle existence of objects in an environment, insects and animals hidden by natural camouflage, and the uses of disguise and illusion are ideas I enjoy working with. Spatial ambiguity has been a common theme through much of my work. I enjoy spatial references that are not quite logical and make me question what is really happening.

The process which I have developed for making my pieces is one which allows me the freedom to work organically in a constant dialogue with materials and imagery. I begin when I have a rough idea of some

*'Beside the Point', 1990. 32½ × 39¼ in (83 × 100 cm). Immersion dyeing with procion dye, airbrush with textile pigments, hand embroidery on cotton. Mounted on acrylic-painted, gessoed canvas*

aspect of the piece. A firm cotton poplin is dyed in liquid procion dye to make the color that I desire. Then a stencil is cut and the initial pattern is airbrushed onto the fabric. Airbrushing allows me to create subtle color changes which add to the spatial illusion in my work. It is done with textile pigments that are heat-set very simply with an iron in a matter of minutes. Iridescent and pearlescent pigments are available now for beautifully subtle special effects. Next, pieces of colored construction paper are cut and pinned in place as a way to design the hand-embroidered areas. These are then stitched, using variations on a few basic stitches – running stitch, satin stitch, long and short stitch – and usually with the fabric stretched tight on a small frame. Shapes are stitched; the new ones are tried in construction paper, moved around, decided upon, stitched in thread, etc.

I continue looking at the piece, adding more shapes in embroidery until it has a certain richness and complexity that tells me it is done. This textile is then mounted on either a stretched cotton fabric or a piece of artist's canvas that has been gessoed and painted with acrylic paint. The painted canvas is a more recent development in my work and allows me the opportunity to extend the design of the textile onto a contrasting material that has a glossier finish.

*'Explosion', 1990. 39 × 47 in (99 × 119 cm). Embroidery on dyed, airbrushed cotton poplin*

# LEE MALERICH

MY IMAGES discuss the relationship between my work and myself, and challenge the outside world. They are, in fact, a super-saturated me – by me and about me. This kind of narcissism is valid only when the personal experience that makes up my image is common to many. Then it becomes some type of sensitive visual therapy that can touch and validate others.

The titles of the works and shapes within the works always have multiple meanings. Perhaps this is one explanation for their kind of feminine universality. The viewer can choose a personal definition.

The symbols and colors change with my emotions. When I am feeling less centered, snakes creep into the images and body parts hook up in chaotic juxtapositions. The tops of heads are sliced off and the contents are released. Shadows are prevalent. I believe that the colors and patterns of my fabrics are mixed in riskier combinations as I mature as an artist.

*'More Than a Consumer', 1991. Image 18 × 18 in (46 × 46 cm), framed 28 × 28 in (71 × 71 cm), detail. Hand and machine embroidery on pieced fabrics*
*The title refers to my wish that women should focus on broader topics in their lives*

'The Queen', 1991. Image 22 × 22 in (56 × 56 cm), framed 32 × 32 in (81 × 81 cm).
Embroidery on pieced fabrics
This title refers to the mother as the barometer of the family's well-being

'Are You?', 1992. Image 18 × 18 in (46 × 46 cm), framed 27 × 27 in (69 × 69 cm).
Hand and machine embroidery and appliqué on pieced fabrics
As the eyes stare out, they challenge the viewer to examine his or her philosophy and biases

The work is a 'stream of consciousness' commentary or challenge to the viewer. If many pieces made one after the other were placed in a line, style and unifying factors would emerge, along with long, slow, compositional developments and basic ideas.

The technical construction of a piece is a painstaking and solitary job. When composing, I turn off the intellect and turn on the emotions. The scale of the pieces of fabric with reference to the whole and color are the important elements here. A fairly straightforward grid construction takes up the central part of each piece – to set a kind of atmospheric tone and begin to carry a color from one intensity to another. When the inside grid is composed, I begin looking at the edges of the grid to determine what will happen to those peripheral colors as they seek the edge of the piece. Something must happen; nothing just 'is'. The fabric constructions, prior to the embroidery, must ride a fine line. They must have character and a definite color commitment, but must not have too much personality. If they do, then the hand embroidery will not add to the whole.

Picking the symbols for embroidery upon the pieced fabric is like playing a card game. Little drawings are dealt out, thrown out, reshuffled and rejected. This part of the compositional process goes very quickly and is fairly accurate in terms of what the piece will finally look like, but it is not carved in stone. Things do change as the tedious hand-stitching process continues. It is during this time that the name of the piece occurs to me. I feel most calm during the hand stitching part of the work and most in control.

Color contributes to the emotion of a piece. The color emerges from a sea of beige. My studio is filled to the ceiling with fabrics, books, magazines, baskets and toys. When I look at my wall of fabrics and my cluttered studio, I am amazed at the lack of color. It is beige chaos. Beneath a small, bright light at the end of one work-table sits the current piece under construction. It blazes out beyond the mass of colorless clutter surrounding it.

Recent work carries very direct challenges. The motif of the two letters 'R' and 'U' poses a question that reverberates through the images. 'Are You?' Are you reacting to the current social/political situation in this country? I continue to ask the question in my work by placing 'RU' in the images whether or not the viewer is guilty of any of the multitude of social *faux pas* we are experiencing today. Are you anti-women? Are you anti-gay? Are you anti-Semitic? These themes reside in my work, because it is difficult to pose them verbally to the guilty parties. And, of course, the question can be posed every time a viewer makes a connection. The finished piece is proof of my existence. It is the vessel through which I voice my opinions and translate what I read, see and hear. It is physical evidence of the heart, mind and soul.

# SYLVIE OLLIVIER

DRAWING AND painting have been part of my life for a long time, and the textile side has become increasingly important.

I used hand stitches until, in 1989, I tried to use my sewing machine and, by experimenting, achieved something closer to what I was unconsciously seeking. For me this livelier style has more movement and makes the fabrics appear to take on an intensive existence; the ground fabric is made more complex by the tensions, the vibrations and the density of the embroidery. For me the visual and tactile pleasures are at one with the movement of machining. The skill involved in manipulating and assembling the fabrics and yarns, and making them communicate, becomes the essential factor in the creation of the magical relationship between a small piece of embroidery and the viewer.

*'Triangle', 1989. 7¾ × 7¾ in (20 × 20 cm). Machine embroidery*

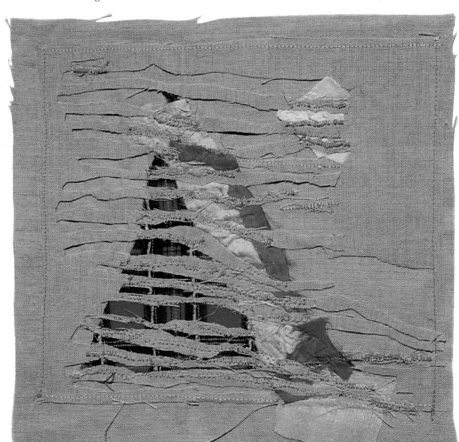

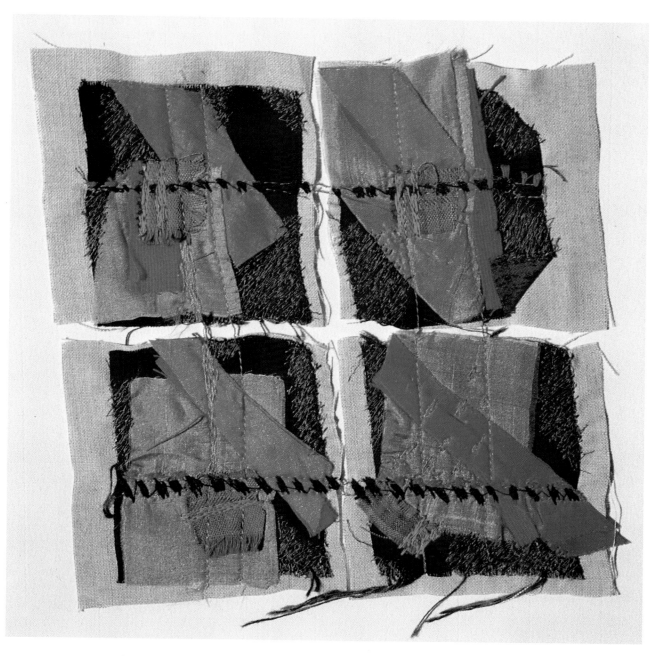

*'Première histoire de quatre', 1991. 7½ × 7½ in (19 × 19 cm). Machine embroidery*

The subjects I work from are varied – linked with nature, with individuals, with my discoveries on more or less imaginary outings. Children's drawings can also trigger strong emotions which I use, like 'La maison de Léonard', a series of embroideries which developed from a drawing by a five-year-old boy. Some embroideries are from wonderful encounters with particular fabrics in more abstract compositions.

On the whole, my embroideries are medium-sized –

8 × 8 in (20 × 20 cm) – or are those of miniature textiles.

The fabrics are always precisely selected, for their brilliant or matt qualities, their transparency, their colour, etc. Then I cut them and, with cotton thread, crinkle them up with lines and whirls on the sewing machine. In a way the embroidery resembles scribbling. The accent is on the intensity of a look at a particular moment.

*'La maison de Léonard-4', 1988. 8½ × 9¼ in (22 × 23 cm). Machine embroidery*

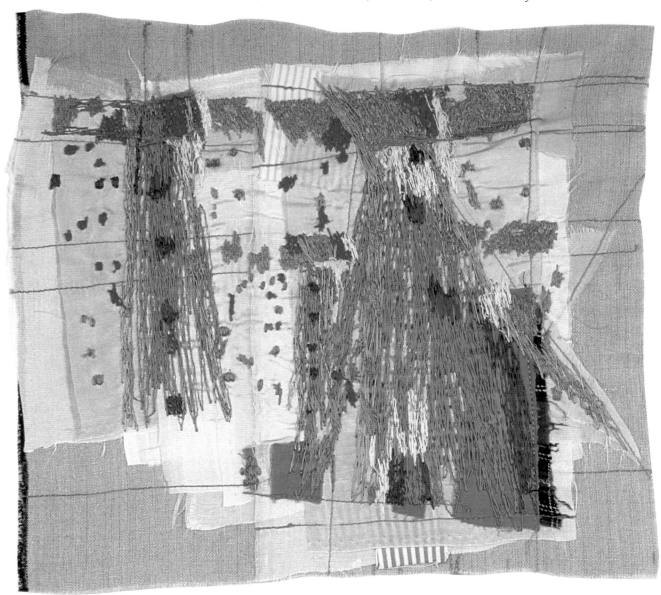

# Heikki Orvola

I AM A ceramics and glass artist and to offset the high-speed decision-making of working with glass I started to embroider. My hands have to have something to do and for me the making of the embroideries, working with my hands, is as important as the final results.

I draw and sketch on odd scraps of paper, frequently the telephone pad, and transfer the outlines to the fabric. Then I choose the colours and stitches. These miniature embroideries are symbols of my free-time interests and demand infinite patience, but I find embroidery relaxing.

It is pure coincidence that my embroidery was exhibited. In an exhibition of my glass work in 1983 some of my miniature embroideries were displayed as a background to the glass pieces. The embroideries aroused admiration and amazement, especially as they were designed and made by a male artist. No one believes me when I say that I embroidered the work myself.

*'The Toys of Louis XVI', 1987. 10½ × 14¾ in (27 × 37 cm). Chain stitch*

A three-year grant by the Finnish State to design miniature embroideries gave me an opportunity to work more intensely on them and to work for an exhibition of just embroidery. However, I felt that I was giving away a very important part of my private life by exhibiting these pieces. I do not work to sell; rather, I do it for my own satisfaction.

I feel my embroideries are characterized by having a spirit of dream-like surrealism. Their forms are spontaneously generated. It is also possible to see my interest in ceramics: I use themes like teapots in my work.

The embroidery is sewn on to the multi-coloured fabric used in fabric-printing (the background fabric used as a pad when printing cloth in the factory). The fabric's multi-coloured patterning comes from the reprinting of various designs on top of each other. This fabric, of random colours and designs, gives an interesting tension to the embroidery, which organizes the chaos of the mechanically made background. The lines of chain stitch are embroidered with silk thread.

One piece of work can take me 200 hours to complete. In the course of three years I have completed thirty pieces. As I have said, for me the making of the embroideries is as important as the final results.

*'Meissen Teapot', 1988. 5¾ × 7 in (15 × 18 cm). Chain stitch*

*'The Lunch in Versailles'*, 1988. 7¾ × 6¼ in (20 × 16 cm). Chain stitch

*'Broken Heart', 1989. 6¾ × 5½ in (17 × 14 cm). Chain stitch*

# TILLEKE SCHWARZ

I LEARNED EMBROIDERY from my mother. I have always liked to do this work and have stuck with it even though it was not 'the thing to do' at an art academy.

I love simple, strong folk art from all over the world and I am especially inspired by samplers. I also find inspiration in daily life. Everything can add to it – some words from a friend, a label in my sweater, a poem. I am not a very philosophical kind of person and most of my work is a direct reaction to my experiences. Through the combination of ideas and emotions, I hope people can project their own feelings into my work, and come up with their own interpretation of it.

*Untitled, 1990. 24 × 29½ in (60 × 75 cm), detail*
*A restful piece in off-whites and with many festive flowers*

'I Have Known Them All', 1992. 21½ × 21½ in (55 × 55 cm)
A contemporary sampler: the texts refer to chicken soup, a Yiddish song, a departure and a typical
advertisement in the New Jewish Weekly, offering a hurricane-proof booth (succah) with a
kosher cupboard (sjach)

I often use traditional motifs in my work; I like to repeat them but change the colour, the material and small elements to create a special rhythm. I combine this with freestyle embroidery and textile paint, and I use little pieces of textiles from my own household, like old handkerchiefs. In 'I Have Known Them All', I have produced a piece about my Jewish background, Jewish culture and the loss of people in the Second World War. The old handkerchief with the blue border reminds me of a table-cloth on Friday nights in a Jewish home.

I start without a detailed plan and find my way while working. Emotions and feelings come without planning ahead or rationalizing them beforehand. The work grows as it progresses and one work contains different thoughts, events, feelings and comments, like a diary. It consists of several layers. Although I might use abstract or stylized elements, the work is mainly figurative.

My favourite fabric is a good-quality linen and the threads are a variety of yarns – linen, cotton, silk and rayon.

The techniques are simple: cross stitch, running stitch, back stitch and couching. I believe that the technique should not be over-emphasized, as too much attention to perfect technique can result in a loss of creativity. I do not make work in series; I find that too boring. Also I put everything I want to say in one piece and then like to start with something new.

*Untitled, 1988. 24 × 20 in (60 × 50 cm), detail*
*A warm red linen inspired by trips to Egypt and Israel. Succulents, cats, diary-notes and*
*a portrait with an undercurrent of traditional peacock and camel motifs*

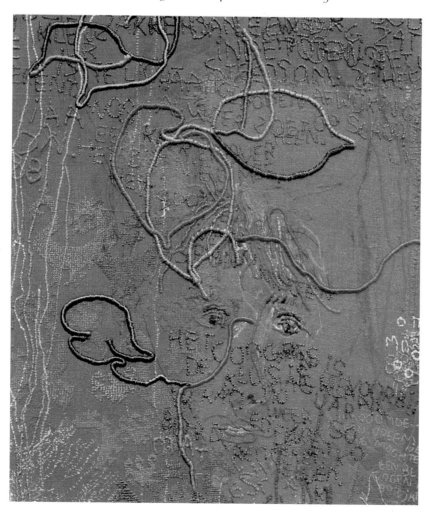

# LYNN SETTERINGTON

M Y WORK, which is of a figurative nature, is inspired to a large extent by my surroundings and environment. The current ideas I have been working on involve the use of utilitarian objects – be they from kitchen, bathroom or garden. I use items that play a part (particularly) in women's lives, but which have been overlooked as mundane and of little value, from cheese-grater to an electric drill or a garden fork. I am interested in the concept of 'beauty in the eye of the beholder' and how this is perceived.

Inspiration for my work also comes from the rich historical and cultural traditions of embroidery and textiles. The change in my recent work was a direct result of seeing a wonderful exhibition of textiles from Bangladesh at the Whitechapel Art Gallery in London. I was particularly drawn to the *Kanthas*, embroidered cloths created from old saris, using the unpicked threads and patched sari cloths to make beautiful new textiles. Likewise, I am drawn to the white on white quilts made by the women of Northumberland and Durham, which, in a different way, use very simple materials and techniques to great effect.

*'D.I.Y.', 1992. 25 × 26 in (64 × 67 cm), detail. Hand-quilted on cotton lawn with cotton thread and polyester wadding*
*This small quilt grew as a direct result of decorating my flat. I was interested in the traditional quilt but wanted to convey a contemporary theme*

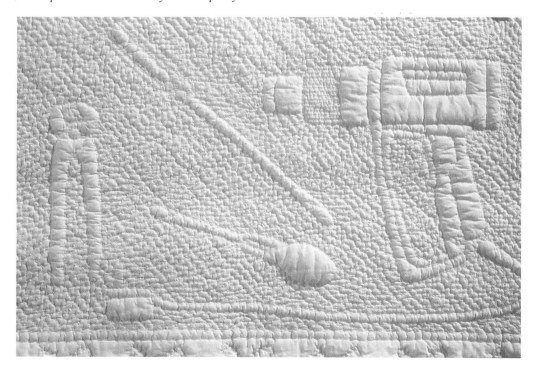

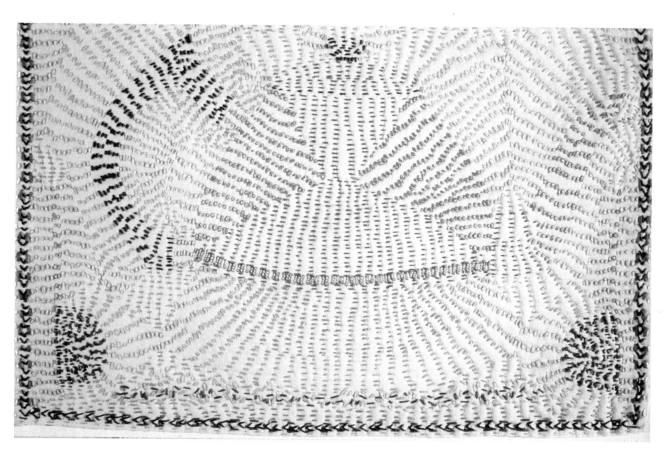

*'Tea Time', 1989. 53 × 13 in (135 × 33 cm), detail. Running stitch through three layers of cotton fabric, using various cotton threads*

*This piece started when I began looking at the various teapots in my flat, but grew to encompass numerous items involved in the process of making tea*

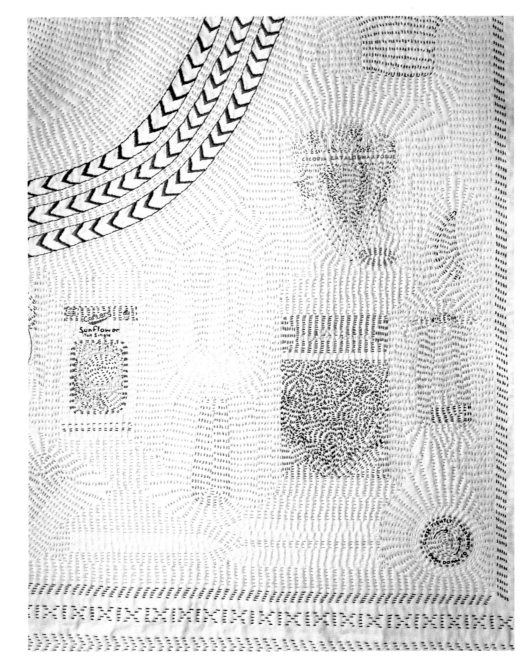

*'Sowing Seed', 1992. 59 × 50 in (150 × 127 cm), detail. Running and seeding stitches in cotton perle and stranded cotton threads. Cotton sheeting fabric*
*Like most of my recent work, this piece is largely autobiographical*

When starting a new piece of work my initial research involves observation and drawing – looking at objects, simple sketching and drawing, trying different combinations and placements that will, in the end, make up the overall format of the embroidery. I also experiment with some sampling in stitch itself, trying different techniques and methods, using different combinations of threads, fabric and colourways. For the last few years at least, my embroidery has been entirely hand stitched. I prefer to work with simple techniques that allow me freedom to express my ideas, while at the same time maintaining a degree of control with the stitching.

My embroideries vary in size and colour according to the function and feel of each piece. I have recently completed a number of large hangings/quilts, the last being 'Sowing Seed'. Begun in early spring, it is a celebration of the beginning of a new season, as well as of my allotment and all that is involved at that time of year. It is also partly a reference to my dad, who taught Rural Science and was a very keen gardener.

I usually work on one embroidery at a time. Each is an individual piece rather than part of a series, although I may return to a theme more than once.

With regard to the materials employed, I use natural fabrics as a ground, normally cotton or linen, in a bleached white. Threads are colourfast DMC or Anchor, either cotton perle or stranded cotton. To transfer images to the cloth I use a combination of stitching an outline of the images in tacking cotton and dissolvable transfer pen. Because the embroidery is quilted through two or three layers of cloth, the finished piece is quite sturdy and I usually machine-wash the embroidery to remove any dirt acquired in the making. I iron the wrong side of the piece, once dry, as the final stage in the process. I do not normally frame or encase my work, firstly because I feel the work is strong enough structurally in its own right, and also to allow the textile to hang naturally and freely and be seen as a tactile object, something very different from a painting or print.

# BARBARA LEE SMITH

I MAKE MY work layer by layer. The substratum cotton fabric begins simply white. I spray-paint textile pigments on one color-layer at a time and they overlap like watercolors. Some areas are masked and left white until almost the end of making the painting, when I apply pure hues. Once painting is complete, it becomes both the source for the forms to be added and the base for the embroidery. The embroidery, always a mix of two hues and two thread textures, reinforces the forms within the painting. I machine with a fine, shiny rayon thread in the bobbin and a sewing-weight thread on the top. The tension is loose, so the lower thread is pulled up to the top, in the form of a whip stitch. In reality the color appears very lively, because I use a slightly different color on the top and in the bobbin, creating a need for the viewer's eye optically to mix a new, third color (sadly, a photograph can't capture this). With changes of light, middle and dark tonal values, yet another dimension is released. I don't think of the stitch as a technique; rather, I see it as a dot or stroke of color and texture.

*'New Corners', 1990. 24 × 41 in (61 × 104 cm). Pigment on cotton/silk.*
*Machine embroidery*
*A stylized page turned down or over reflects my interest in writing and reading and the adventures of the mind around every 'new corner'*

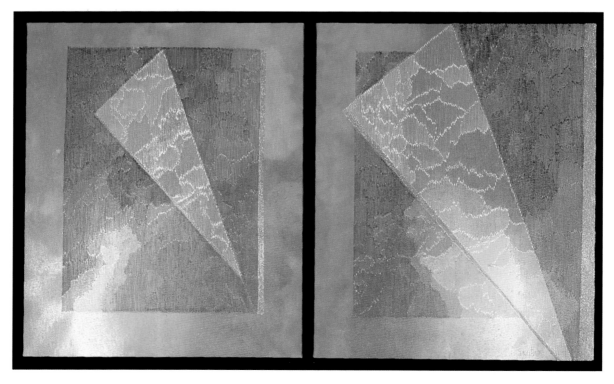

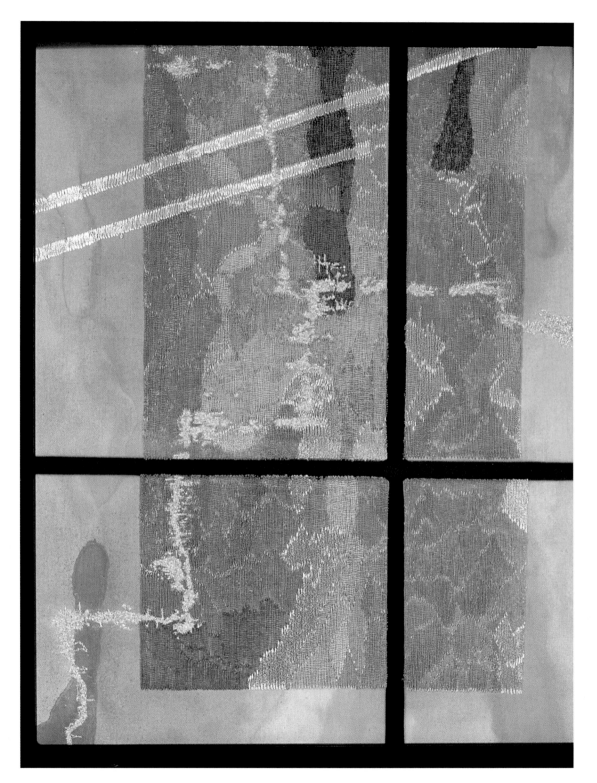

*'Two Lights', 1989. 48 × 48 in (122 × 122 cm), detail. Spray-painted cotton and silk fabric, metallics brushed on painting, machine embroidery (whip stitch) with metallics, rayons and other threads*

*A continuing exploration of structures we build that relate to nature led to a series of studies of windows*

*'Where Did the Words Go?', 1992. 42 × 21 in (107 × 53 cm). Spray-painted cotton with textile pigments, metallic pigments scraped over painting, machine embroidery (whip stitch) with metallics, rayons and other threads*

*After three years consumed by writing a book on contemporary North American embroidery, I wondered if I would be able to return to making art without the support of words, hence the title*

Just as the process of making the work is one of adding on in order to reveal, so my ideas behind the work overlap. In some works windows are suggested, framing light and providing transparent effects, as well as allowing me to explore ideas of inside/outside, concealing/revealing and man-made/natural. In others a triangular form suggests a page being turned, expressing my involvement with words and love of books. A new image appears in a series of bridges. Colors and painted or stitched lines bridge each module, visually connecting them. Based on photographs I've taken in Scotland and Chicago, a more literal representation of a bridge is stitched into such works.

I aim for the finished work to appear as if it were made all in a moment. In actual fact, I squeeze studio time in between desk work: writing, filing slides and teaching. I learned long ago that there is no such thing as a 'typical day'. My work day starts around 6.30 a.m. and goes on to about 4.30 p.m. However, no matter what I am doing, there is a part of my brain that is always tuned in to the ideas I want to express. I make notes and sketches wherever I am, some of which I'll develop later, while others perform as a sort of mental art-aerobics. I enjoy most the times when I can just play with new art materials, techniques and ideas.

With the exception of experiments, I prefer to work on a large scale. I remember Constance Howard's advice in a class, 'Work large. You will see your mistakes faster', and I must have taken that to heart. Using modules to form a single piece allows for technical flexibility. The spaces between each module – usually 1 in (2.5 cm) – also integrate the wall material with the work.

Any idea worth exploring I do in a series. Sometimes I will drop an idea only to find it resurfacing, like an old friend one hasn't seen for some time, years later. Image, color, form, idea, technique, materials and mental attunement must balance to create a work. Like constructing a bridge, each element must be in perfect tension and alignment with the next to form a single, working totality.

# Rose Marie Szulc

Each piece I do begins with an 'idea', a starting point or theme to reference for a story, which I carry out utilizing text and/or pictures. Initially, I spend lots of time reading, drawing and formulating my ideas – a gestation period. My inspiration is mainly derived from popular culture – music, street life, films and magazines, then and now – with a heavy dose of feminist politics, art stories, philosophy and psychology. It is a very personal statement, yet it also has collective implications. What is true for me is often true generally. I believe that one of the artist's many roles is to inform and educate, to expose hypocrisy and poke fun at the pretentious. A sense of humour is imperative, as is the ability to laugh at yourself. I love comics and the conventions inherent in that medium. I often feel that we live in a comic-book world of super-heroes and masks, odysseys and tasks; truth is generally stranger than fiction.

*'Truth', Panel 1, 'Unpalatable Truth', detail*

*Panel 1, detail*

*'Truth', Panel 4, 'Truth Does Count', 1991. 80 × 80 in (200 × 200 cm), detail*

My jottings, in whatever form they take, are then translated into working plans for pieces if they are to be carried out in a textile form (I work in a variety of media). I usually draw to scale, something like map-making, then I take the map apart and piece the work together like a jigsaw puzzle.

I am interested in patterns, layering and story-telling, as a metaphor for the real world. I am not hung up on technique for its own sake, but I believe that if you are charging high prices for your work, it has to be both curatorially sound and value for money. Thus a good understanding of technique is very necessary, but it should not preclude creativity or stop you from doing things you want to do.

I aim to produce work that is understandable and approachable for the general public but which additionally offers deeper insights for those prepared to read the hidden messages. There is a code in life and in artwork: honour should have 'u' in it.

'Truth' is comprised of four panels, each measuring 80 in (2 m) square, with a total length of 319 in (8 m). Materials used are cotton fabric and threads, resin-bonded pigment, print paste and laundry-markers. Techniques involved drawing, painting, printing, reverse and surface appliqué and machine stitching. The work is highly coloured and quite fluorescent. It took over a year to make, with time off to do other smaller pieces and earn a living (everyone knows you can't make a living as a textile artist!).

# Anna Torma

I DEFINE MYSELF as a textile artist and I frequently choose to express my thoughts and feelings by means of embroidery.

I learned the techniques of needlework from my mother; it was an unwritten rule in my village in Hungary that every girl had to know how to embroider. At the time I thought of this as an imposition, because I wanted very much to be 'modern'. Since then, however, I have discovered that I unwittingly inherited something from the community's tradition which I am now able to pass on.

*'Everyday Poems', 1992. 52 × 45 in (132 × 114 cm), detail. Cotton fabric and satin-stitch hand embroidery*

*'Oasis', 1989. 30 × 31 in (76 × 79 cm). Satin-stitch hand embroidery on cotton fabric*

'Feast', 1991. 59 × 35 in (150 × 89 cm), detail. Velvet, cotton, lace and ribbons. Satin
stitch, hand embroidery

There have been certain periods in my life when I was unable to work consistently, but even in these difficult times I none the less continued with my art. This was the situation when my two boys were small children. We also had to wait in a refugee camp in Germany for a considerable period before we finally emigrated to Canada in 1989. It has taken me a while to become acquainted with Canadian life. Now, after a period of adjustment, I feel revitalized.

Embroidery has imposed itself on my life, but now I feel that I am in control of my work, rather than my work controlling me. The very demanding and precise traditional stitching allows me to produce classically beautiful flowers. Stitches lend themselves to a certain rhythm, which also allows me to describe graphically the innocence and imagination of children.

I work mainly on cotton fabrics with threads that I often dye myself. I use satin stitch and running stitch. In 'Feast' I used lace and ribbon for ornamentation. This piece shows my fascination with Catholic feasts which take place in the countryside in Hungary, with flags, flowers and people singing old sacred music around the church. Times have changed; the Madonna is not beautiful in the old way any more. This piece is my reconciliation of Catholic, pagan and modern myth.

Planning my work always involves a drama. I take a central theme (human, animal, plant) and a variety of motifs become entwined. Some say my work is jarring, but I want to be able to express my innermost dreams and desires.

I hope to show in my work the contrast between the representation's harshness and the beauty and content-ment expressed in the intricate details of embroidery.

# D. R. WAGNER

I USE EVERYTHING, from the daily newspaper to comic books, from opera to photographs I take myself. As I work mainly in narrative, I tend to use a lot of different sources in each picture. For instance, my most recent large piece, 'The Fulfillment of Prophecy', uses sources as varied as a 1943 issue of *Life* magazine, a 1452 manuscript in the Vienna Library, drawings of Tibetan 'seed' symbols that are related to the function of actually 'making' sound, some of my own poetry and other drawings I had friends do for me specifically for the work.

I am fortunate in that I am able to work in a number of disciplines: I write poetry, make music, draw, paint, make sculpture and enjoy working with other artists. My inspiration probably comes from when I wake up and realize 'here I am' in this incredible world. To create is the best. If one can do this, then, I feel, one must.

*'The Fulfillment of Prophecy', 1991. 16 × 34 in (41 × 86 cm). Triptych.*
*Cotton, Balger and Lurex*

I love a story. I love mystery. I love to have to question why something is in a picture. I also feel strongly that the work must reveal something about itself when first looked at. The image must capture the viewer at some level, otherwise why look at the thing? I also feel, however, that one shouldn't explain the whole thing anyway. To really get into a piece of work, something should happen to the viewer – an interior dialogue; make up another story using these images. I would rather be involved with a piece of art myself than ask the artist to tell me *why* everything in the piece is as it is.

My approach always varies. Sometimes I know exactly what the picture will be. That can change right in the middle of work. It is a kind of encounter with self that is initiated by the thinking which goes on its own path. I'll draft drawing after drawing and then suddenly change the piece if I feel it isn't working. The question is how to remain open to the process – the creative process – while one is stitching away. For me, I've developed the hare-brained idea that the work actually progresses rather quickly and I surprise myself with every few stitches by how the work looks.

I work on twenty-five-point canvas, in different colors, depending on the piece. I use four strands of embroidery floss. I mix my colors from the entire range of those offered, but will use other brands if I need them. I also use Balger blending-filament for special effects, as well as Lurex. I have recently begun using light-reactive Balger filament to gain certain special effects, such as having some images visible only in ultraviolet light. This allows me more depth of meaning for those who care to pursue the work further. It also allows me to layer other factors into the picture without cluttering it up. I also use overstitching, generally back stitch, to outline or emphasize an area or a detail of something.

The work ranges from pieces which are very tiny – 1 × 2 in (2.5 × 5 cm) – to ones about 10 × 36 in (25 × 91 cm). It is sometimes hard to determine what size a piece is going to be, because I am prone to change my ideas while working. To finish, the work is blocked, wrapped around museum board (acid-free) and mounted using a heat-reversing product called foto-flat. It is also a neutral product.

*'The Fulfillment of Prophecy', detail of central panel in ultraviolet light*
*The three figures in the foreground are, left to right, Richard Tauber, a famous tenor of the*
*thirties and forties, Jarmilna Novotna, a famous Czech soprano and international beauty, and*
*Franz Lehar, composer of* The Merry Widow

'The Dark Side of the Moon', 1990. 12 × 15½ in (30 × 39 cm). Cotton, Balger
This piece uses light-reactive filaments in one of the palm trees and in the text panel, which tells
us that when changes come to art, almost no one notices. It is like the changing of the moon

'La Cruz y la Musica', 1991. 5⅝ × 8¾ in (14 × 22 cm). Cotton, Balger, luminous Balger on canvas

The light-reactive portion is actually derived from a photograph of Annie Taylor, the first person to challenge Niagara Falls in a barrel and survive

# VERINA WARREN

Nᴀᴛᴜʀᴇ's ᴍɪɴᴜᴛɪᴀᴇ are the source of my inspiration, landscape in all its multifarious ways – from the formality of garden structure and plant growth to the wider aspects of land, sea and sky.

Living and working in a rural environment have taught me to be constantly aware of the significance of even the smallest changes in the landscape. How often have I admired those past recorders of time, for keeping such detailed notes, often accompanied by sketches, of all they observed. I still find the descriptive written word evocative and when applied to landscape, it becomes very inspiring.

*'Bordered by Beauty of Amaranthine Grace', 1989. 12 × 17 in (30 × 43 cm). Machine embroidery on silk painted background*
*Borders within borders; unrestrained herbaceous bed contained within a formal, stylized border; interpretation of walled gardens*

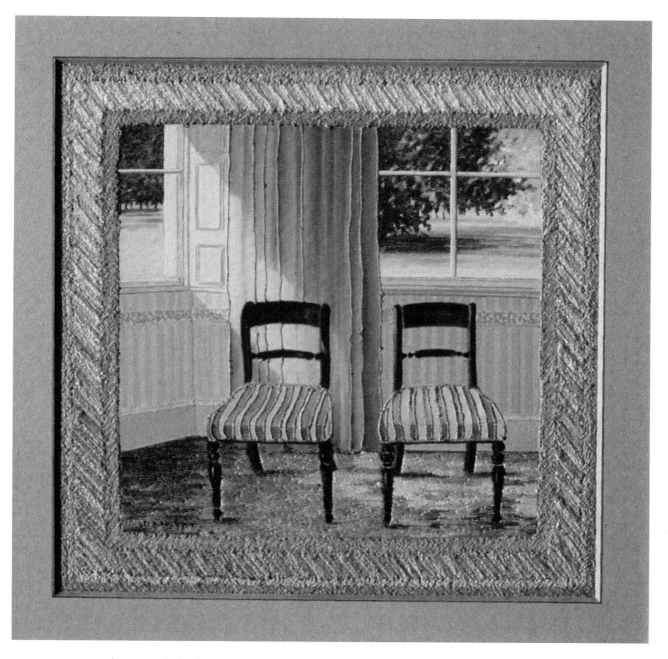

'Lit Within by Sunlight and Peace', 1992. 7½ × 7 in (19 × 18 cm). Machine-embroidered
silk fabric, painted or airbrushed with dye
Sunlight creating warmth on a carpet; the quiet peace of a sunny afternoon

With that in mind, I've been able to observe with more clarity, on my daily walks, the subtle changes taking place as season replaces season – changes in plant growth, colour, light and shade, patterns evolving and fading. These are the things that move and motivate me and continually encourage me to pursue an often difficult path as a freelance textile artist.

What I have discovered to be the true essence of my work finds its base in colour – the mark-making element of colour used to create form and structure. It is the colour within a landscape that first holds my attention, then its shape and line.

Certain outside factors often need to be considered before embarking on a new work; client and commission dictates, exhibition venues, even the country can all effect changes. Certain lines of verse or passages of music can influence the final finished design, its aspect, colour and harmony relating to words and sounds while the original concept arose from direct observational imagery.

My approach to my work has certainly undergone a fundamental change and while I feel that I am only at the beginning of this change, one aspect has been clarified, and that is technique. When the work was of a small scale, the machine technique of whip stitch was very relevant. Now that the coloured mark is what I seek to achieve, the stitch used must not detract from the finished surface. It is the interaction of fabric, stitch and colour that now holds my interest.

I prefer to use silk for my backgrounds because light plays such an important part in the work and the quality of silk is such that the play of light can be affected. I buy my silk by the bale, directly from wholesalers, and colour it accordingly, using silk dyes. Free machine embroidery is used to create a mark in texture. Texture is the difference between fibre art and painting. It adds another dimension to the surface, especially when combined with painting. I use paint and dye and thread in conjunction, one with the other. Once some initial colour has been applied, I then concentrate on blending and building tonal relationships, adding thread and paint where applicable.

I have always used painted borders, initially as this helped to bridge the gap between 'art' and embroidery. It enabled me to sell my work through galleries, as an accepted art form, at a time when most embroideries were relegated to 'craft venues'. Now painted borders have become an integral part of my work – no arbitrary decoration but a means of extending the visual parameters or conversely concentrating and emphasizing the areas of embroidery. They create a variety of surface and depth and give a personal dimension and statement to the work. The final presentation of a finished piece must be as complete and professional as the work itself.

# MARTEL WIEGAND

For several years I have been working with the same technique, a kind of Mola work. I buy fabrics and dye some cottons myself, then I put three layers of fabric on top of each other and use this as a base. I work freely on the machine, knowing the idea I want to produce, and once this has been achieved, I cut between shapes with my scissors to the second and third layers of fabric. I cut out on both sides of the fabric; the front and the reverse of the fabric are equally important. I machine, cut and machine again, until I feel the work is complete.

*'Nanuna', 1992. 16 × 9 in (41 × 23 cm). Textile object*
*Cotton fabric, machine embroidery, cut work*

The pieces of fabric that are cut out I use again in other works, and in this way I produce a series. The small pieces are about 16 × 12 in (40 × 30 cm), the larger ones up to 275 × 47 in (7 m × 120 cm). With works like 'Flag for Animals', I make the pieces separately and gradually put them together to produce the whole thing.

I am not interested in telling stories but rather in using subjects like heads, people, animals, ships, water, structures and tools as signs. The dark and light qualities in my life appear as signs which are realized especially through the sensitive materials. I feel my work will always change because the fabrics are soft and move – a reason why I like to work in this method.

'Flag for Animals', 1989–90. 149 × 47 in (378 × 119 cm), detail
Cotton fabric, machine embroidery, cut work

# ALEXA WILSON

Vᴵˢᵁᴬᴸ ᴬᴺᴰ physical experiences found in different natural environments are the source of my inspiration. I am moved by soft, gentle forms and natural colours depicted through hills, fields, sand, sea, trees, animals, etc. Natural rhythms and movements in land formations create interest and present subtle relationships with colour, surface and shape.

My work goes to the furthest limit of pure abstraction without abandoning the traditional convention of working from nature. It tries to define the qualities of landscape and life depicted in subtle nuances of tone, colour, surface and shape, forming relationships which set up a gentle interaction within the finished textile. Movement and shuttling rhythms direct the eye across the work but are always checked, resolving chaos into order to maintain a visual harmony.

*'Indigo Straws', 1989. 22 × 18 in (56 × 46 cm). Mercerized cotton thread, ikat dyed with synthetic indigo. Parallel threads are stiffened with PVA, applied over wooden dowels and attached to a calico backing. Indigo wooden discs are threaded to the end of the rods*
*Inspired by field and furrow, movement is directed across ordered parallel lines. The horizon, skyline, keeps in check direction and composition*

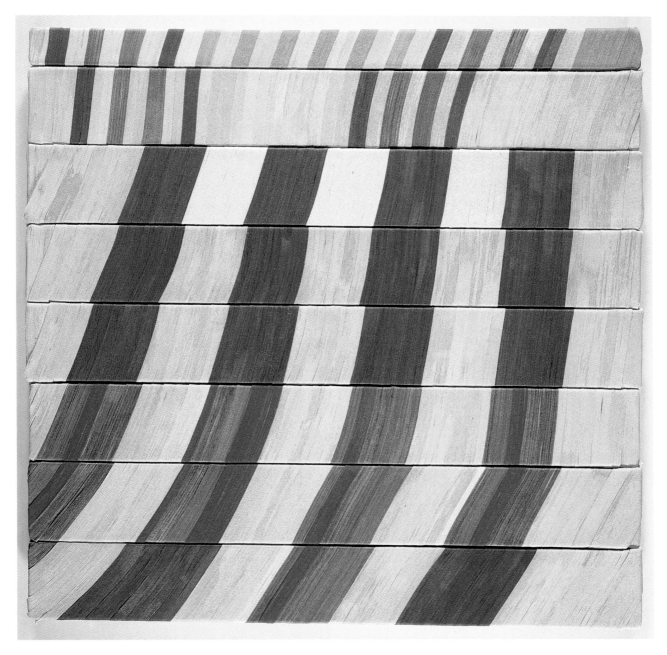

'Blue Striped Field', 1988. 22 × 18 in (56 × 46 cm). Mercerized cotton threads hand-dyed, stiffened and bonded together to form ribbon-like braids. Braids are attached around various widths of foam board and laid down in horizontal lines

I rely on drawing and painting to capture forms that represent my impressions of nature. I employ sensuous colours – blues, greens, pinks and yellows – layering a mixture of media and gouache, acrylic, inks, procion dye and hot wax to achieve the desired effect. My textile work is not directly translated from completed drawings but from areas of surface, colour and shape that capture the essence of emotion.

The selection of suitable yarns, materials and their colouring for a finished piece is of vital importance. I use both natural and chemical dyes, combining several techniques – space, dip and ikat dyeing. Silk, linen, cotton, raffia, sisal and wool are favourable working materials, as they have natural inherent qualities that respond beautifully to the natural and chemical dyes. Chosen yarns are often applied with PVA, wax or paper pulp to achieve a stiffened effect.

Before starting a textile piece I will experiment with mixing yarns – thick and thin, lustrous with full, fibrous with smooth. I incorporate both hand and machine embroidery techniques, such as couching, wrapping and canvas work. As I trained as an embroiderer and weaver, I often use 'designed yarns' with both embroidery and weave techniques, as each process contributes equally to the effect of the completed textile.

'Blue Striped Field' was inspired by a field beside a beach in Cyprus. The cobalt-blue sky reflected down on to the sandy soil, with a soft breeze directed across. The materials used were mercerized cotton threads hand-dyed, stiffened and bonded together to form ribbon-like braids. Braids are attached around various widths of foam board and laid down in horizontal lines.

# INEZ ZÜST·GERICKE

HEN I started to embroider in the early 1970s (being an industrial textile designer and also a painter), I wanted to be seen as an answer to what I called 'pollution in art' – which meant using square miles of canvas and gallons of paint to produce a work of art in practically no time. In contrast to this, embroidery calls for a lot of metaphysical things like concentration, thought, mind, time, perseverance, skill, hope, etc. and very few physical ones (thread, canvas, needles). I still feel this is a better way to reflect the needs of our times, rather than imitating the consumer society, as has happened in the fine arts. Gradually I became fascinated by embroidery *per se* and, parallel to painting, developed it as a means of expression.

*'Lyric Quartet', detail: '3 Refrains'. Silk embroidery on wool. 4 single forms = 4 sets of words.*
*3 repetitive forms = 3 refrains, distinguished from and also related to each other by colour*

'Lyric Quartet', 1987. 39½ × 39½ in (100 × 100 cm). Silk embroidery on wool
Poetry visualized by embroidery; organic materials set between inorganic acrylic-glass plates to
become legible

The research work I do is rather intellectual, trying to visualize, in as many ways as possible, fundamental design ideas, such as basic geometric forms, their combination, their rotation. I always calculate their surface area, which has to be either equal in all forms within one work or in specific proportion to each other. Other fundamental design ideas are all contrasts: multi-coloured versus monochrome, black-and-white versus colour, systematic organization versus random – ideas which can be visualized in an infinite number of ways, a real fund of research.

I think that my need to organize colour and form is rooted in a desire to rearrange the world, to prove it is possible to live in a contradictory world with contrasting cultures and still form a whole where everybody and everything has her/his/its essential place. Of course, there is not just one way to achieve this aim but many; hence my series or pairs. I myself agonize about pollution and injustice, the egotistical plundering of the south by the north, the demolition of our natural resources, nature itself.

I try to make my technique sensible and self-evident. I try not to embroider an idea I could paint more easily. I try to use embroidery as a means of expressing my ideas, with the basic fabric as a form-giving element (its woven structure or, with tulle, its hexagon guides my stitches). I cannot sketch my embroidery beforehand in detail, but I sketch part of it on checkered paper, or I base outlines directly on the fabric. I determine the general colour scheme before I start and usually select the shades while working. My embroideries tend to be in half-cross stitch. I use cotton DMC mouline thread, six-fold, or silk buttonhole silk-twist Nm 40/3. The hours I spend are innumerable.

*'Equal – Unequal', 1990. Each panel 19¾ × 19¾ in (50 × 50 cm). Cotton and silk embroidery on nylon tulle, between acrylic plates*
*A two-piece work visualizing the general design principle 'positive – negative' both in form and colour. Form: either roaming freely or using strict weaving-patterns. Colour: any shade of colour versus black and white*